# ELIZABETH GO

Elizabeth Goudge was born in Wells, Somerset in 1900, died in 1984. Her father was a Canon of Ely Cathedral and his work in the theological colleges at Salisbury, Wells and Ely, and later as Regius Professor of Divinity at Oxford, established the locations for her early home life, later the settings for many of her novels.

She taught handicrafts before her writing began to be published. Her first major success was *Green Dolphin Country* (1944), which won her a Literary Guild Award in the United States and was subsequently filmed. She gained a large and devoted audience of adults and children for this and her other much-loved novels, which include *The Dean's Watch*, *A City of Bells* and *Towers in the Mist*, and the novels of the Eliots of Damerosehay. *A Vision of God* includes poetry she wrote towards the end of her life, which was not published in book form.

'Few novelists have had comparable knowledge and faith in the goodness of human nature, the beauty of childhood and the pursuit of things lovely and of good report.' *The Times*

# CHRISTINE RAWLINS

Christine Rawlins has loved the writings of Elizabeth Goudge for many years. She writes, 'I wanted to produce this anthology because I feel that one of her greatest strengths as a novelist is her insight into human frailty and the inner struggle for faith. Faith would appear to be an ongoing pilgrimage of discovery, and I like the way Miss Goudge seems to have looked to writers and thinkers of many denominations and creeds in her search for truth.' Married with one young son, Mrs Rawlins lives in Kent.

SPIRE

## Books by Elizabeth Goudge

*Novels*
Island Magic
A City of Bells
Towers in the Mist
The Middle Window
The Bird in the Tree
The Castle on the Hill
Green Dolphin Country
The Herb of Grace
The Heart of the Family
Gentian Hill
The Rosemary Tree
The White Witch
The Dean's Watch
The Scent of Water
The Child From the Sea

*Short Stories*
White Wings
The Reward of Faith
The Well of the Star
The Pedlar's Pack
The Golden Skylark
The Ikon on the Wall
The Lost Angel

*Novelette*
The Sister of the Angels

*Juveniles*
Smoky House
Henrietta's House
The Little White Horse
Make-Believe
The Valley of Song
Linnets and Valerians

*Non-Fiction*
God So Loved the World
St Francis of Assisi
A Diary of Prayer

*Anthology*
At the Sign of the Dolphin
A Book of Comfort
A Christmas Book
The Ten Gifts
A Book of Faith
A Book of Peace

*Omnibus*
The Eliots of Damerosehay
The Cathedral Trilogy

*Autobiography*
The Joy of the Snow

# A VISION OF GOD
## A Selection from the Writings of Elizabeth Goudge

### edited by Christine Rawlins

SPIRE

First published in Great Britain 1990

Spire is an imprint of Hodder & Stoughton *Publishers*

Bible quotations are from the Authorised (King James)
Version, the Good News Bible and the New English Bible

**British Library Cataloguing in Publication Data**

Goudge, Elizabeth, *1900–1984*
A vision of God: a selection of the writings of Elizabeth
Goudge
I. Title    II. Rawlins, Christine
828.91209

ISBN 0-340-52457-X

*Printed in Great Britain for Hodder and Stoughton Limited, Mill Road, Dunton
Green, Sevenoaks, Kent by Clays Limited, St Ives plc. Photoset by Rowland
Phototypesetting Limited, Bury St Edmunds, Suffolk.*

*Hodder and Stoughton Editorial Office: 47 Bedford Square, London WC1B 3DP.*

# CONTENTS

*Introduction*                                                  7

Part I        I am the Light of the World                      11

Part II       I am the Way                                     21

              1   Love                                         23
              2   Service                                      34
              3   Prayer                                       39
              4   Childlikeness                                47
              5   Suffering                                    54

Part III      I am the Truth                                   63

Part IV       I am Life                                        75

Part V        Poems                                            89

# Introduction

One struggles with thoughts and words, and then suddenly they all fall down like the cards with which a child has laboriously tried to build a house, and lie there in chaos at one's feet. For we know nothing. The mystery of the universe and of our tiny breath of being is too great for us.

*The Joy of the Snow*

Elizabeth Goudge's struggles with thoughts and words, her sensitivity to the mystery, created a vision of God which shines out from her books like a great light. As *The Times* said of her, 'few novelists have had comparable knowledge and faith in the goodness of human nature . . . the pursuit of things lovely and of good report'.

Countless readers have discovered within her books this atmosphere of pure goodness, of such a clarity that beauty, truth, love of God and his Creation, are almost tangible; have discovered, in effect, her own personal faith. She said of this gift, in *The Joy of the Snow*,

Perhaps unconsciously, and without knowing it, we want to share our faith and what it has done for us and to make contact with those who think as we do. I say unconsciously because in my own case when a book comes into my mind it comes simply as a story; personal belief is something that comes in apparently without my knowledge or contriving. But I think it is this latter

7

unintended thing that makes the strongest link between reader and writer. We all hold our faith with a certain amount of fear and trembling (even Blake wrote, 'My hand trembles exceedingly upon the Rock of Ages') and to find that others share our faith has a steadying influence, especially in these days when the Rock of Ages himself is for ever being prodded and sounded to see if he is still there. To those of us who think the tapping hammers would not sound so loudly if he was not there the likemindedness is a very special joy.

Hers was a developing faith, a vision that grew and matured during many years of writing. For example in 1951 she published *God So Loved the World*, in which she said, 'Hell is not a child's nightmare but reality. It exists. It is possible to go there, and a great many of us will go there'; *The Joy of the Snow*, however, tells us that by 1974 she had 'let go of the horror of eternal punishment' and had come to 'believe that in the old sense of the word there is no hell'.

She knew that, whatever growth and fresh insight we acquire, the mystery is still too great for our understanding. And yet, despite the humble assertion that her struggles to understand produced only chaos, there is a constant theme at the centre of all her writings which forms the heart of her vision of God. From her earliest novel to the mature vision of her autobiography, the central importance of unity, reconciliation, *one-ness*, is reiterated; for she came increasingly to see everything in life, even the darkness of fear and pain and suffering, as part of the one perfect whole that is Creation, that tiny hazelnut of Dame Julian's vision that was all that is made.

The only thing that is not part of the perfection is the evil that men do, which Elizabeth Goudge recognised as emanating from man's denial of one-ness; from the separation caused by concentration upon the self and the refusal to acknowledge unity with God and our fellow men. And yet, with her ever-present delight in paradox, she saw that even the suffering of separation was a thing that united mankind.

> They were together in what they suffered, caught in this lunatic age that was not of their making. Or had they made it? While one of them harboured one thought of hatred, hugged to himself one moment of self-indulgence, they were not guiltless of the misery of these times. Mutual guilt locked them together, as well as mutual sorrow . . . Wicked though the times might be, never in the history of the world had one man's life been so interwoven with that of another. What men felt to be the meaningless writhing of the whole interlocked surface of human affairs was a sort of mockery of what union might be; of what it was down in the depths where the selfless had union with each other and their God. A mockery and a signpost at the same time.
>
> *The Heart of the Family*

In this same novel of the postwar years comes also the recognition that it is not only with God and mankind that we must acknowledge one-ness, but with the whole of Creation.

> Holding a child in your arms gave you much the same feeling as pushing your finger down into the earth when you were gardening, or having your horse nuzzle the palm of your hand for sugar. Quite suddenly you felt that your life was not an isolated thing, but existed in all other lives, as all other lives existed within yours. There wasn't anything anywhere to which you could say, 'We don't need each other.'

Now, more than thirty-five years since the publication of those words, we know them to be true; we have discovered to our horror that selfishness in mankind can throw into disharmony the whole symphony of creation. In his arro-

9

gance, man has always believed himself to be the central theme of that symphony, but Elizabeth Goudge appears to have thought otherwise.

The dependence of men upon the creatures to whom they considered themselves superior filled her with delight. Animals, birds and flowers could live very satisfactorily without men, but men deprived of the creatures perished miserably.

*The White Witch*

But Christ said, 'Whoever believes in me shall not perish', and Elizabeth Goudge saw that the path to unity was the way of Christ, the way of love, service, prayer, humility and shared suffering. And so these extracts from her writings have been grouped together to illustrate some of the teachings of Christ the Way, who is himself One-ness, the unification of life and death, master and servant, God and man.

In one life only had the fighting, the healing, the teaching, the praying and the suffering held equal and perfect place ... The Word now taught and healed, fought and suffered, through the yielded wills of other men ...

Thinking this there gradually came to him complete and utter comfort in the thought of the one-ness of all men with each other and their God. Of all the illusions which torment the minds of men one of the worst is the illusion of separateness.

*Gentian Hill*

# Part I

# *I am the Light of the World*

'Whoever follows me will have
the light of life and will never
walk in darkness.'

*John 8:12*

## SEPARATION

God had cried out over the darkened earth, 'Let there be light!'

... But man had flung up his arm across his eyes that he might not see the light, had turned his back on the garden of his inheritance, had stumbled out of it and killed his brother. And now he was always fighting. That poor stumbling fool who had covered the eyes and raised his hands against his brother was at war for ever with the man who had talked with God in the garden in the cool of the evening, had called the animals by their names and known his brother as bone of his bone and spirit of his spirit. Only a legend, that story of the lost garden, but something of the truth must lie hidden in it, for one had only to look at oneself to see those two men who are the same man, fighting down the ages, the one a rebel for ever, the other straining back always after the lost inheritance. And the conflict in the individual soul spread out and out, like ripples on the water, to nations and creeds and classes, till one was deafened and sickened by the clamour, mad and afraid.

*The Castle on the Hill*

## ONE-NESS

The problem of evil ... will always remain one of the most disturbing mysteries of the universe for both our hearts and our minds. A full understanding of the suffering of God's creatures ... presupposes in us an appreciation of the nature and

13

value of 'participated being' which, for lack of any point of comparison, we cannot have.

*Le Milieu divin*, Pierre Teilhard de Chardin

We cannot understand – not yet – but we can see how the more we lose our sense of separateness in the knowledge of the one-ness of all living creatures, millions of small leaves on the one single tree of life, the more we shall lose our sense of self-importance, and so be liberated from our self-pity; a bondage so horrible that I believe it can bring us at last to a state not unlike that of Gollum, the dreadful creature Tolkien created, living alone in the dark, talking to himself, murmuring, 'My preciouss. My preciouss.'

But if that 'my preciouss' were to be the song of the leaves on the tree, each leaf delighting in all the others, there could be no love of self, no hatred and no sin, and none of the suffering that springs from sin. And since a tree has no voice but the wind, and the leaves know it, they would soon know who it was who was singing their song with them and through them, and lifting and swinging them in the dance. If we can find a little of our one-ness with all other creatures, and love for them, then I believe we are half-way towards finding God.

*The Joy of the Snow*

O Lord Christ, lifted on the cross that you may draw all men unto you, have mercy upon us. It is our self-love that crucified you then, and crucifies you now in every thought that turns in upon self, passing you by, in every word and deed that pierces and thrusts for self, wounding you in your children. Longing for you we yet stand far off upon the hill of Calvary, mourning for what we are, afraid of the darkness we have brought about us by what we do, clinging still to the secret sweetness of self-love, and unable to

14

bring it to the love that burns for us upon the cross that it may die there in the flame. Lord, strengthen our weak longing for you with the great strength of your longing for us, and bring us through the darkness to where you are.

*A Diary of Prayer*

## COUSIN MARY'S VISION OF THE NATIVITY

I had fallen asleep at last and drifted into nightmare. I was imprisoned in stone. I knew then what men suffer who are walled up alive. But I was able to think and I thought, Shall I scream and beat against the wall or shall I keep my mouth shut and be still? I wanted to scream because it would have been the easier thing. But I didn't. And when I had been still for a little while I found myself slowly edging forward. There was a crack in the stone. The hardness pressed against me upon each side in a horrible way, as though trying to crush me, but I could edge forward through the crack. I went on scraping through and at last there was a glimmer of light. It came to my feet like a sword and I knew it had made the crack, a sword of fire splitting the stone. And then the walls drew back slightly on each side of me, as though the light pushed them. I had a sense of conflict, as though the darkness reeled and staggered, resisting the light in an anguish of evil strength. It had a fearful power. But the light, that seemed such a small beam in comparison with that infinity of blackness, kept the channel open and I fled down it. There was room now to run. I ran and ran and came out into the light.

I had escaped. I was so overwhelmed with thankfulness that I nearly fell. I sank down on the ground and sat back on my heels, like children do sometimes when they are saying their prayers and are tired. It was ground, not stone, it was a floor of trodden earth. The stone walls were still there, but the light had hollowed them out into a cave and they no longer frightened me. There was a lantern in the cave and people were moving about, a man and woman caring for a girl who lay on a pile of hay. And for a new-born child. As I watched the woman stooped and put him into his mother's arms. An ox and ass and a tired donkey were tethered to the wall of the cave, and their breath was like smoke . . . It was like one of the nativity scenes that the old masters painted only not tidy and pretty like those. The girl was exhausted, her clothes were crumpled and the sweat on her face gleamed in the lantern light. The man was dusty and tired and not yet free of the anxiety that had been racking him for hours past. The woman was one of those kindly bodies who turn up from somewhere to lend a hand in times of human crises. She made soft clucking noises as she gave the baby to his mother, and the two women gave each other a long look of triumph before the girl bent over her baby. He was like all new-born babies. He looked old and wizened, and so frail that my heart nearly stopped in fear, as it always does when I see a new-born child. How could anything so weak survive? His thin wail echoed in the stony place and then was stifled as he sought his mother.

They've not come yet, I thought. All the prettiness the artists painted isn't here. No angels, no shepherds, no children with their lambs. It's stripped down to the bare bones of the rock and the child. There's no one here. And then I thought, I am here, and I asked, who am I, Lord? And then I knew that I was everyone. I wasn't solitary. Everyone was me and I was everyone. We were all here, every sinner whose evil had built up those dark walls that held the child like a trap. For looking round I saw that the cave of the nativity was very small. The walls were pressing in upon him close and hard and dark like they pressed in on me. And the old claustrophobic terror was back on me again, but not for myself. I remembered the rocks of the wilderness and the multitude of sinners surging in, selfish and clamorous, sick and sweaty, clawing with their hot hands, giving him no time so much as to eat. I remembered the mocking crowd about the cross and the thick darkness. I remembered the second cave, the dark and stifling tomb. Two stony caves, forming as it were the two clasps of the circle of his life on earth. And I remembered Saint Augustine saying, 'He looked us through the lattice of our flesh and he spake us fair.' Shut up in that prison of aching flesh and torn nerves, trapped in it . . . The Lord of glory . . . I remembered the sword of light that had split the rock of sin, making for me the way of escape to where he was at the heart of it. At my heart. At the heart of everything that happened to me, everything I did, everything I endured. He was not the weakness that he seemed for he had a sword in his hand and all evil at last would go reeling back before it. He had entered the prison house of his own will. And so he was not trapped and nor was I. There was always the way of escape so long as it was to the heart of it, whatever it was, that one went to find him.

*The Scent of Water*

## CHRIST CASTING OUT DEVILS

The sight of him at close grips with such evil had a very disturbing effect upon some of those who saw it. Their own idea of holiness was of something withdrawn, something that drew back its skirts from contamination, whereas Our Lord, who did not have ideas about holiness but just was holiness, plunged down into the middle of the evil that he might rescue its victims.

*God So Loved the World*

To grow in holiness is to grow in the power of turning from yourself to God and his children. When there is no more turning back to yourself, that wounding of the soul of the world, then you are whole.

*The Child from the Sea*

# WILLIAM THE HUNCHBACK'S VISION
## OF THE CRUCIFIXION

William . . . was not only hunchbacked but, as the old book says, 'mightily misshapen, with short bow legs and long arms that hung down, sickly and very plain of countenance', so much so that . . . children were scared of him, or laughed and threw stones. And he himself, neglected as he was by the uncle whom he lived with and knocked about by his horde of healthy children, grew to be as scared of the human race as a hunted leveret . . .

He went into the woods and lived there alone for some months . . . Then one day in early spring he suddenly appeared among the stonemasons who were enlarging the abbey church and with changed and smiling countenance offered them his services, and laboured with them until the work was completed. Then with the same cheerful face, quite changed from the man he had been, he presented himself before the Abbot and asked that he might be accepted as a lay brother . . . He lived until old age, dying just before the dissolution of the abbey and was reckoned at the time of his death to be a very holy man. He himself however deemed those mistaken who called him holy, declaring himself to be a great sinner saved from despair only by the mercy of God that came upon him in the vision in the wood.

He delighted to tell this story and believed implicitly in his vision. When it was suggested to him that he had imagined what he saw, he said, dream or vision, what did it matter? Whichever it was his God had by its means lifted him out of his despair. He had, he said, that afternoon in early spring, taken shelter in the barn from a sudden drenching thunderstorm. Around sunset the rain ceased and he went outside to get himself a drink of water from the well under the thorn tree. He came out into a dazzle of gold and to the east, where the last of the storm clouds made a violet bruise in the sky, there was a rainbow. The trees were rosy with the swelling buds and the

grass sparkled. The birds were singing and the first prim-
roses were in bloom around the well. Yet there was no
lightening of his darkness as he stood looking at them,
only a deepening of it. Caught in this web of beauty he felt
himself a thing of horror, ugly and dirty in body, mind and
soul. He wished he could tear himself out of the shining
web, that he might no longer defile it. And then the
thought came to him, why not? On the other side of the
well was the thorn, a young tree but with stout branches,
and inside the barn there was a length of rope. For a short
while after he would continue to defile the web and then he
would be found and buried and the fair earth would be quit
of him.

He looked hard at the tree, seeing it already as his
gallows, and then found that he could not look away.
There were no green leaves yet to veil the starkness of it, it
was still a winter tree, and the thorns looked long and
sharp. He looked deeper and deeper into the tree, into the
heart of it, trying to see himself hanging on the tree, and
presently, with horror, he did. And then, staring as though
nothing of him now existed except his straining eyes and
thundering heart, he knew it was not himself but another.
And he knew who it was. He would never, afterwards,
attempt to describe what he saw. He could not. But he did
say that he believed the fair Lord of life had accepted a
death so shameful of deliberate intent of love, so that
nothing that can happen to the body should cause any man
to feel himself separated from God. And he said further
that fearful though the sight was it was not what he saw
that made him cast himself down upon the ground, with
his face hidden in the grass, and weep. It was that the Lord
of heaven, giving himself into the hands of men, that is to
say into his hands, to do with what he would, had by his
hands been broken. This he said he had never sufficiently
considered, and now, considering it, his heart broke. A
little later he was able to stop weeping and lifting himself
up from the ground he dared to look again into the heart of
the tree. It was as it had been, a bare winter tree full of

19

thorns. But he knew now that he need never hang there, since another had chosen to hang there in his place, ridding the world of his ugliness by taking his sin into his own body that it might die with him. For he saw now that his true ugliness had been withdrawn by his Lord while he wept. His misshapen body remained, but men would not again shrink from him. What they had shrunk from had been his own sin of self-hatred, that had made him like a beaten cur in their presence. Why should he hate himself, since God had loved him enough to die for him? He would go back into the world, and smile at all the folk in it, and love them with the same love, and they would no longer shrink from him . . . He held out his hands and looked at them, remembering how they had treated his Lord. He would make reparation, now, to those other men who mysteriously were his Lord, with his hands. But that was not enough. The least he could do, he, Adam, the man who had so brutally done what he would when his trusting Lord put himself into his hands, was now to put himself into his Lord's hands to be done with what his Lord willed. He held out his hands towards the tree, empty to his human sight yet containing all he was, and said aloud, 'Into thy hands'.

*The Scent of Water*

## Part II

# *I am the Way*

'If you obey my teaching . . . you
will know the truth, and the
truth will set you free.'

*John 8:31–2*

# 1

# Love

'Love one another, as I have loved you.'
*John 15:12*

*'Love will never come to an end'*

Only in the manger and upon the cross is love seen in its maturity, for upon earth the mighty strength of love has been unveiled once only. On earth, among men, it is seldom more than a seed in the hearts of those who choose it. If it grows at all it is no more than a stunted and sometimes harmful thing, for its true growth and purging are beyond death. There it learns to pour itself out until it has no self left to pour. Then, in the hollow of God's hand into which it has emptied itself, it is his own to all eternity.

*The Dean's Watch*

*Love. The only indestructible thing. The only wealth and the only reality.*

*The Dean's Watch*

In the spring of 1939 my father died . . . The nurses . . . told me I was wasting my time, sitting so many hours by

the bed of a dying man who would never regain conscious-
ness. But he did. He appeared to come back from some
great distance and said slowly and distinctly, 'Dear one, it
is loving that matters,' and then drifted away again upon
the great peaceful journey. So that is the end of it for these
great men. All their accumulated knowledge, all the argu-
ment and controversy, seem of little importance. Only love
remains important and is immortal. Baron von Hugel was
much like my father in his dying for his last words to his
niece were, 'It is caring that matters. It is caring.'

*The Joy of the Snow*

### 'Love is kind'

Compassion . . . He saw now that it was the very first
necessity, always and everywhere, and should flow between all men, always and everywhere. Men lived with
their nearest and dearest and knew little of them, and
strangers passing by in the street were as impersonal as
trees walking, and all the while there was this deep
affinity, for all men suffered.

*The Dean's Watch*

If we could all see the hidden wounds of others . . . 'Love
your enemies' would not be so hard a command to keep.

*The White Witch*

### 'Love . . . envies no-one'

## MRS ROGERS

I don't think she ever envied the good fortune of others
because I think she never realised that her own life was a

hard one. When she compared herself with other people it was always with compassion for them . . .

Thinking of her, and of the greatness of her example, I think one of the saintly qualities is this unconscious refusal to envy the lot of others. For the unselfish, envy is an impossible exercise anyway since it is destructive; a symptom of a hidden urge to smash and destroy, while love is bound up with the urge to create and give; even if there is nothing to give except compassion . . .

Perhaps what the world needs is more compassion, more and more of it, not for human beings only but for every single living creature whose small span of life and enjoyment can be shattered by the lack of it.

*The Joy of the Snow*

*'Love is never selfish'*

## MRS BELLING CHOOSES SELF-LOVE

Between sleeping and waking she heard Baba whimpering under the bed and felt a momentary stirring of something like compunction. She swung on a dark tide, but not overwhelmed yet, because the compunction bore her up just once more. Suspended between one world and another, she remembered dimly that there had been other times when some weakening of self-love had lifted her up like this to abide the questioning, the detested probing questioning. 'Whom do men say that I am? Whom do men say that I am?' She had always refused even to consider an answer, struggled to get away from the intolerable claim made upon her, fought to get back to her ownership of herself. The questioning now was childishly simple, not the question which had been like the thundering of a great wave along a beach, but a gentle question put to a child. 'Won't you call the little dog out from under the bed? Won't you call the little dog out from under the bed?' Swinging in

25

darkness on the dark tide, she saw him quite clearly, shivering on the floor, a paw that had been hurt in his fall doubled under him, blood oozing from the corner of his eye where her ring had cut him, an obese unpleasant little dog who loved her and had tried to lick her hand. But it was too much trouble to drag herself out of sleep and call to him. Why should she? She was just getting warm and comfortable. Let him stay there. 'No,' she said.

*The Rosemary Tree*

We all of us need to be toppled off the throne of self . . . Perched up there the tears of others are never upon our own cheek.

*The White Witch*

To every human being the pain of perhaps not having love returned is less important than the blessed fact of loving.

*The Joy of the Snow*

Requited love gets as much as it gives, but unrequited love gets nothing for itself and so it must be the best sort of love that there is.

*The Castle on the Hill*

## MISS WENTWORTH

Looking back over the years . . . she realized more sharply than she had ever done that the exclusiveness of her caring had been a sin in her . . . Looking back on one's life at the end of it the perspective was changed and one saw things differently. At the beginning she had prided herself upon the fact that longing to be alone with Richard she had nevertheless faithfully done her duty by Charles and his boy, now she saw that to have kept all her love for Richard had been no virtue. Richard . . . being a part of her, loving [him] had merely been loving herself. To have loved the other two would have been true love; they had needed love just as badly, and she could have given it to them if it had occurred to her to ask for the grace of God. But she had been too self-confident in those days to realize her own bitter need and poverty, and perhaps too proud to cast herself in her lovelessness upon God's mercy if she had . . . Her own past pride she regarded now as the worst sin of her life.

*The Rosemary Tree*

## 'Love is not proud'

Proud folk separate themselves from others, judging them . . . To criticize others we must hold them from us, at arm's length so to speak. And then, before you know where you are, you've pushed them away and you're the poorer.

*The Rosemary Tree*

'Familiarity breeds contempt . . .' How vile is this tendency to belittle loveliness just because you are used to it. We live with lovable people and instead of reverencing their nobility we rivet our whole attention upon their faults . . . It is pride; we like to feel superior to, or at least on an equality with, the people about us, and if we were to start paying attention to their great and good qualities we soon should not.

*God So Loved the World*

*'Love . . . does not gloat over other men's sins'*

The sins of the flesh . . . The founder of his faith had handled such matters gently, reserving the divine wrath for pride, hypocrisy or oppression of the weak.

*The Child from the Sea*

*'Love keeps no score of wrongs'*

After the cross, I think that what most convinces us of the love of God is the forgiveness of the greatest of his sons and daughters. I do not think that love and forgiveness can be separated, since real love by its very nature must forgive. To know oneself forgiven by God and by those we love, is a most humbling and lovely experience and teaches us the necessity for forgiveness. The power to receive some hurt done to you, great or small, with the forgiveness that lets it come to an end in you, puts an end to retaliation, that horrible eye for an eye, tooth for a tooth business that can keep some impulse of cruelty circling round the world for ever.

*The Joy of the Snow*

Forgiving others should not be difficult, knowing as we do how great is our own need of it, but forgiving oneself is another matter.

*The Joy of the Snow*

28

We think about the harm we do until we become monsters in our own eyes. That is good, you'll say; but we think about the monster until he has us circling about him as though he were some hideous little heathen god. If it stops there it can become almost a form of devil-worship, and it is not worship the devil in us needs.

*The Heart of the Family*

There is no one harder to forgive than oneself; it can take years. Nevertheless we know inside ourselves that it must be done, for remorse is a sin that rots away the very vitals of the soul. And we know well the price of a soul to God. If God and his saints in their divine foolishness put such a price upon our soul we should not let it rot.

*The Joy of the Snow*

'Love never gives up'

To love God subtly alters a human being. If the simile is not too homely the lover of God has glue in his veins and tends to be more adherent than other men. The more he loves God the more, for God's sake, he sticks to his woman, his job or his faith. Christians should be judged, I think, by their stickableness, since by that alone can God get anything done in this world; that appears to be disintegrating now before our horrified eyes from sheer lack of glue.

*The Joy of the Snow*

'It is love, then, that you should strive for'

I had not known before that love is obedience. You want to love, and you can't, and you hate yourself because you can't, and all the time love is not some marvellous thing that you feel but some hard thing that you do. And this in a way is easier because with God's help you can command your will when you can't command your feelings. With us, feelings seem to be important, but he doesn't appear to agree with us.

*The Scent of Water*

To a certain extent we are all actors, and we must be. We must wear the mask of courage however afraid we are and we must perform the actions of love however loveless we feel, but . . . it may be that the mask will bite deep, the actions shape and probe like the hands of a sculptor on clay, and we shall actually become braver and more loving.

*The Child from the Sea*

Lord, we thank Thee for all the love that has been given to us, for the love of family and friends, and above all for your love poured out upon us every moment of our lives in steadfast glory. Forgive our unworthiness. Forgive the many times we have disappointed those who love us, have failed them, wearied them, saddened them. Failing them we have failed you, and hurting them we have wounded our Saviour who for love's sake died for us. Lord, have mercy on us, and forgive. You do not fail those who love you. You do not change nor vary. Teach us your own constancy in love, your humility, selflessness and generosity. Look in pity on our small and tarnished loving, protect, foster and strengthen it, that it may be less unworthy to be offered to you and to your children. O Light of the World, teach us how to love.

*A Diary of Prayer*

*One should love and never be afraid. One should love everyone, everything.*

*The Child from the Sea*

## MISS MONTAGUE

What should she do . . . ?

She never knew what put it into her head that she, unloved, should love. Religion for her parents, and therefore for their children, was not much more than a formality and it had not occurred to her to pray about her problem, and yet from somewhere the idea came as though in answer to her question, and . . . she dispassionately considered it. Could mere loving be a life's work? Could it be a career like marriage or nursing the sick or going on the stage? Could it be adventure? Christians were commanded to love, it was something laid upon them that they had to do whether they liked it or not. They had to love . . . But what was love? Was there anything or anybody that she herself truly loved?

A rather shattering honesty was as much a part of her as her strong will and her humour, and the answer to this question was that she loved the cat and Blanche's bower . . . She was concerned for them both and had so identified herself with them that they seemed part of her. Making a start with the cat, was it possible to make of this concern and identification a deliberate activity that should pass out in widening circles, to her parents and the servants and the brothers and sisters and their families, to the city and its people, the Cathedral, even at last perhaps to God himself? It came to her in a flash that it must be wonderful to hold God and be held by him, as she held the cat in her arms rubbing her cheek against his soft fur, and was in turn held within the safety and quietness of the bower. Then she was shocked by the irreverence of her thought, and tried to thrust it away. But she did not quite succeed. From that day onwards it remained warm and glowing at the back of her mind.

So she took a vow to love. Millions before her had taken the same simple vow but she was different from the majority because she kept her vow, kept it even after she had discovered the cost of simplicity. Until now she had only read her Bible as a pious exercise, but now she read it as an engineer reads a blueprint and a traveller a map, unemotionally because she was not emotional, but with a profound concentration because her life depended on it. Bit by bit over a period of years, that seemed to her long, she began to get her scaffolding into place. She saw that all her powers, even those which had seemed to mitigate against love, such as her shrewdness which had always been quick to see the faults of others, her ambition and self-will, could by a change of direction be bound over in service to the one overmastering purpose. She saw that she must turn from herself, and began to see something of the discipline that that entailed, and found too as she struggled that no one and nothing by themselves seemed to have the power to entirely hold her when she turned to them.

It was then that the central figure of the gospels, a historical figure whom she deeply revered and sought to imitate, began at rare intervals to flash out at her like live lightning from their pages, frightening her, turning the grave blueprint into a dazzle of reflected fire. Gradually she learned to see that her fear was not of the lightning itself but what it showed her of the nature of love, for it dazzled behind the stark horror of Calvary. At this point, where so many vowed lovers faint and fail, Mary Montague went doggedly on over another period of years that seemed if possible longer and harder than the former period. At some point along the way, she did not know where because the change came so slowly and gradually, she realized that he had got her and got everything. His love held and illumined every human being for whom she was concerned, and whom she served with the profound compassion which was their need and right, held the Cathedral, the city, every flower and leaf and creature, giving it reality and beauty. She could not take her eyes from the incredible glory of his love. As far as it was possible for a human being in this world she had turned from herself. She could say, 'I have been turned,' and did not know how very few can speak these words with truth.

*The Dean's Watch*

# 2

# Service

'Go, and do thou likewise.'
*Luke 10:37*

What of those many loving people who do not find God?
Are they in this world deprived of Christ? I think the
answer is again in the cross. Wherever there is suffering,
there they find him, and with or without recognition that
is always where the greatest men and women do find him.
Francis of Assisi, Father Damian, Elizabeth Fry, Albert
Schweitzer, these and many other Christians knew that
they found Christ in those whom they served and acknowledged that the love they felt was God's love in them, but
those who do not know do the same work for the same God
and have a richness and fulfilment in their lives unknown
to many so-called Christians. I know of one, a man who has
suffered the impossible things, war, grief, torture and
imprisonment, and come through uncorrupted, with a
compassion so strong that wherever he may be in the
world he must find his way to those who suffer most, no
matter how terrible their suffering or how dreadful the
place where they are, and keep them company, and serve
them as far as he is able.

*The Joy of the Snow*

Love must give or it is not love.

*Saint Francis of Assisi*


## THE FEEDING OF THE FIVE THOUSAND

If we imagine . . . the little boy holding his basket out to
Our Lord, and Our Lord taking from it the five loaves and
two small fishes and making of them enough to feed a
multitude, we see a picture of the wonderful way in which
he takes the very little that we have to give him and uses
it; it may be almost nothing that we have to give, yet he
takes that nothing into his hands, blesses it, and makes it
enough for the purpose for which he wants it.

*God So Loved the World*


*'Anything you did for one of my brothers here, however
humble, you did for me.'*

*Matthew 25:40*


Over and over again, with endless patience, in story
after story, in sentence after sentence . . . Our Lord
teaches us that when we say unkind things to each other,
criticise each other, persecute and kill each other, when
we refuse to help each other, we are doing these things to
God. And when we serve and love each other, are gentle
and pitiful and courteous, it is God whom we love and
serve . . . But still we can't seem to learn that lesson, even
though we know there is no hope for us until we do.

*God So Loved the World*

O Saviour of the world, teach us how to pray for those who are lost in desolations of darkness without the knowledge of the mercy that is yourself. We remember the innocent victims of war and all the agony they suffer, those who are sunk in the wretchedness of sin and can find no deliverance, those in despair, those beset by temptation, those who are greatly afraid, those who have been overwhelmed by torment of mind or body. Save us from the cowardice that would turn away from the thought of these things, from the indifference that would pass them by. Give us penitence for the evil in ourselves which has added to the darkness of the world, and if there be any small thing we can do to lighten any misery, show us what it is and help us to do it. Teach us how to pray with the compassion which is not afraid to suffer with those who suffer and, if need be, to enter into darkness with them. O Everlasting Mercy, who once in time came from the height of heaven down to the depth of our need, come again in power to forgive us and renew us and set us on fire, that through the labours and prayers of broken-hearted sinners your mercy may banish the darkness and bring new life upon the earth.

*A Diary of Prayer*

Conversion is sterile unless one can face and implement the paradox of Christ. He is God and a man on the gallows. His voice is the beauty of the world and the crying of a hungry child. He is peace in our hearts and conviction of sin. He draws us to him with tenderness and then says the most uncomfortable things to us. To go through the gospels and note them all is a frightening experience.

Hypocrites that are like whitewashed tombs, which make a fine show from without, but are full inside of dead men's bones and every kind of filth . . . Harlots have the lead of *you* on the road to the Kingdom of

God . . . I was hungry and you did not feed me; I was thirsty but you did not give me drink; I was homeless and you did not bring me in; naked and you did not clothe me; sick and in prison and you did not visit me . . . Hear the truth . . . In so far as you did not do these things to one of these little ones, you did not do them to me.

I believe that the converted can face a great danger. It is when the skill of Christ has brought us to him we forget about his children in concentration about himself . . . But Christ won't be concentrated upon in this one-sided manner. He won't have us on these terms. He is completely identified with all suffering creatures and we have him with them, or not at all. It can come about that some man or woman finds God not by way of a sense of unity with his children but through a journey lonely as that of the Prodigal Son, but I believe that if we go home like the Prodigal Son we must go out again as the Good Samaritan.

I feel myself that I have come really to know this too late and I understand what my father felt when towards the end of his life he said (and it was the only time when I ever saw him close to weeping), 'When I come to the end I shall be saying to God, "Let me go back and try again."' Was it simply a cry of penitence or did he feel at last as I do now, that one life on this earth is not enough to satisfy the hunger that we have to serve him in all the ways that are open to us under earthly conditions? One earthly life may have been enough for Christ, so perfectly balanced was he, so entirely concentrated on the matter in hand, yet able to turn from one thing to another as though there were no difficult transitions between storm and calm, teaching and healing, praying and going to a party, suffering and dying, but all were the one smooth flow of the music of the will of God.

But we are torn and exhausted by the trivialities and conflicts of self, by stress and strain and busyness. Those who are devotedly serving their fellow men are often too tired to pray, creative artists are so absorbed in the world of their own creativity that the tiny place assumes enormous proportions and they are in danger of forgetting the suffering world outside; and in proportion as they forget their own world darkens. Only the contemplatives seem in better shape, for their prayer has no walls. It embraces all the world and all the people in it and all their pain. They tell us that their deep prayer actually shares the pain and so to those of us to whom prayer goes no deeper than 'the conscious occupation of the praying mind, or the sound of the voice praying', such prayer seems a frightening thing. Nevertheless it has the music and if in old age we feel heartbroken because we know that we have failed Christ in his suffering children it is not too late to try and reach out to them in that life of selfless prayer. Death may come upon us before we have done more than merely try to reach out, but it will not matter too much. I believe that death interrupts nothing of importance if the goal is Christ.

*The Joy of the Snow*

# 3

# Prayer

'Ask, and you will receive . . .
knock, and the door will be opened to you.'

*Luke 11:9*

Prayer is the greatest activity there is . . . It is directed
not only to the praise of God but to the redemption of the
soul of man . . .

Bringing men to re-birth He works . . . through the souls
that are offered up to Him to be the channels of His will.

*The Rosemary Tree*

## HARRIET'S PRAYER

Since she had had to lead this shut-in invalid life she
had found illness involved suffering almost as much from
the tyranny of painful thoughts as from physical pain.
Outside this lovely valley where she lived the world was a
dreadful place and first one misery would possess her mind
and then another. Crimes against children would take
hold of her one day, and on another she would be grieving
for the blind or mad. She lacked the physical strength to
thrust tormenting thought from her even if she had

wanted to, but she did not want to. The fortunate, she thought, and she counted herself fortunate, should not insulate themselves in their good fortune. If they could do nothing else they could pray, and she prayed as she was able, grieving over the childishness of her prayer but trying to make it real to herself by letting the travail of her mind bring forth one concrete fact at a time to pray about; one child in danger, some particular man in darkness, some particular prisoner facing the world again with fear and shame; God knew who they were even if she did not.

*The Rosemary Tree*

## JOHN WENTWORTH'S PRAYER

Perhaps, if he faced the truth, he would find that one of the reasons why he spent so much time in prayer was because the results of prayer were unknown and one could indulge in the sin of wishful thinking. For it most certainly was sin for a man to sit back picturing the pleasing results of his prayer. Unless prayer was bread cast upon the waters in blind faith, without hope or desire for knowledge or reward, then it was nothing more than a selfish and dangerous indulgence of fantasy.

*The Rosemary Tree*

## PARSON HAWTHYN'S PRAYER

Slipping once more to his painful knees he tried to pray . . . and this time as he struggled to compose his thoughts, they ceased to wander, were gently taken hold of and spun together, as it seemed, into one thread that tautened and drew out into a shining line of wonder. He crawled up it as a spider might do, taking those for whom he prayed with him, though aware that in his case the line was not of his own spinning, up and up while the wonder deepened into joy, and the joy into worship. He hung for what seemed a timeless moment upon the point of worship and then the thread snapped, and he fell, so heavy was the weight of his sin.

*   *   *

The apparent failure of prayer never disturbed him, convinced as he was both of its hidden worth and of the adorable perfection of the will of God . . .

'Failure? How can I fail when I am nothing? There is but one power that is our own . . . the power to offer the emptiness that we are, and we make idols of ourselves if we think we are the only instruments of salvation ready to God's hand.'

*The White Witch*


## THE DEAN'S PRAYER

There was . . . that power that had been given him of taking hold of an evil situation, wrestling with it, [and] shaking it as a terrier shakes a rat until the evil fell out of it and fastened on himself. Then he carried the evil on his own shoulders to the place of prayer, carried it up a long hill in darkness, but willingly. Each time he felt himself alone, yet each time when the weight became too much for him it was shared, then lifted, as though he had never been alone. Yet if there had been no hope of help he would still have been just as willing. But in that mystery nothing was his own except the willingness.

*The Dean's Watch*


## THE OLD CURATE'S PRAYER

Love, your God, is a trinity. There are three necessary prayers and they have three words each. They are these,

'Lord have mercy. Thee I adore. Into Thy hands.' Not difficult to remember. If in times of distress you hold to these you will do well.

*The Scent of Water*


## HILARY'S PRAYER

One day, with great difficulty, I suddenly put into practice and knew as truth what of course I had always known theoretically, that if pain is offered to God as prayer, then pain and prayer are synonymous. A sort of substitution takes place that is like the old story of Beauty and the Beast. The utterly abominable Thing that prevents your prayer becomes your prayer. And you know what prayer is . . . It's all of a piece, the prayer of a mystic or of a child, adoration or intercession, it's all the same thing; whether you feel it or not, it is union with God in the deep places where the fountains are. Once you have managed the wrenching effort of substitution, the abominable Thing, while remaining utterly detestable for yourself, becomes the channel of grace for others, and so the dearest treasure that you have . . . It's a deliberate and costly action of the will. It can be a real wrenching of the soul. Yet the more you practise it, the fresher and greener grows your life.

*The Heart of the Family*


## JEAN ANDERSON'S PRAYER

Last night, longing for some sunlit hours . . . she had prayed that it might be fine again. Her brother said it was childish to pray about the weather because it obeyed the immutable laws of nature. God did not go messing about with his own laws and she was only wasting her time. But it confused her to try and think what she could pray about and what she couldn't. She had to pray about everything or she couldn't live, and it was surprising how the fine days came, and the cat had her kittens safely and she was able at all times to obey.

'Look out of the window.'

She obeyed. Huddling her dressing-gown about her she drew the curtains and looked out. From her high east window she could see over the garden to the country beyond. The sky was veiled in silver and swathes of mist lay over the fields. The trees and the quiet cattle stood knee-deep in it but the lifted crests of the trees were illumined, as though some glory was preparing. She watched as the mist thinned and brightened. She did not cease to watch yet when it happened her eyes had not been able to observe the moment of miracle. All she could say was that the sun had not been there and now it was, a ball of pale gold hung like an apple against the silver sky. Suddenly every blade of wet grass below her, every leaf and twig-full of crystal lanterns, caught on fire and the robins began to sing. For a few moments the sun was hers and then with grateful joy she gave it back to him again.

*The Scent of Water*


When the clock strikes, or however else you shall measure the day, it is good to turn to God, that the returns of devotion may be the measure of your time. And do so also in the breaches of your sleep. You do not even need to speak. To turn is enough.

*The Child from the Sea*


## MISS MONTAGUE'S PRAYER

She said, I will learn to pray.
It was a promise . . . and she whose prayer until now had

43

been the murmuring of soothing and much loved words in the tired intervals between one thing and another, or the presentation to Almighty God of inventories of the needs of the city . . . abandoned herself for the sake of those she loved to silence and the dark, understanding however dimly that to draw some tiny fraction of the sin of the world into her own being with this darkness was to do away with it.

*The Dean's Watch*

The quietness of that threshold of heaven . . . is always there for us, like an old church porch in a street where the traffic thunders by, if only we can manage to forget ourselves and our busyness for long enough to become conscious of it, to get out of the traffic and go in.

*Saint Francis of Assisi*

Go in. Go down the stony passage that leads to the cave at the heart of the world that is also your own heart. He is there . . . and he is the peace of the world, and the joy of the world, and all that is . . . And what he is, no man knows.

*The Child from the Sea*

## STELLA'S MEDITATION IN THE STABLE

Stella had not outgrown her childhood's sensitiveness to colour, scent and sound. The orange glow of the lantern, the warm velvety shadows of the stable, the contented purring of the cats and the breathing of the oxen, the smell of the clean beasts and the hay, seemed to weave themselves together and make for her a cloak of warm tranquillity. Wrapped in it she lay still, reaching down inside herself for that deep peace in which her being was rooted like a tree. Awareness of that peace gave her the deepest happiness that she knew. Sometimes it came, as now, like a deep echo of outward tranquillity, like a bell ringing far under the sea in answer to some church bell on the earth, and those were the moments when it lasted, but she had known it come also in moments of trouble and stress, though it was no more then than a touch, gone in a moment yet sufficient in strength to steady one for much longer than its moment of duration . . .

She shut her eyes . . . She was sinking down and down through depth upon depth of peace, the green water closing over her head, but she was not afraid . . .

'If I take the wings of the morning, and remain in the uttermost parts of the sea, even there shall Thy hand lead me, and Thy right hand shall hold me . . . Whither shall I go then from Thy Spirit, or whither shall I go then from Thy presence?'

. . . The presence was the peace and the peace was the presence. If you could only sink down deep enough to find it there was no separation . . .

*Gentian Hill*


## MARGUERITE'S MEDITATION

Like Brother Lawrence she had learned by bitter experience that 'useless thoughts spoil all', and that nothing so thoroughly ousts the presence of God as talking to oneself. Through years of hard mental discipline, carried on with homely unseen heroism, she had learned to silence the chatter of self, to focus her mind in meditation, until the beauty dwelt upon became not a picture but an opening door, and then with sealed lips but open ears to go away through it by her secret stair to God. From that place she came away again with power and laughter in her soul, and with her natural clarity so burnished that she could radiate them through its clear transparency . . .

In old days she had felt as though the laughter and strength that she brought away from her hours of prayer had flowed out from herself, and the knowledge of her own power had delighted her; now she knew that they flowed only through her, and what delighted her was the miraculous power of God that could pick up even an empty straw and make it the channel of His grace. Such a glorious and loving condescension had called out the love of her whole being, prostrated in humility, and to it she had surrendered herself utterly and forever. 'Intreat me not to leave thee, or to return from following after thee.' That was the true cry of love, born of humility, and it had liberated her from the burden of her own selfhood and unlocked for her the gate of Paradise.

*Green Dolphin Country*

# 4

# Childlikeness

'Turn round and become like children.'
*Matthew 18:3*

'Verily I say unto you,' said Our Lord . . . 'whosoever shall not receive the kingdom of heaven as a little child, he shall not enter therein.'

He was reminding his disciples of something that he had said upon another day. 'The kingdom of God is within you.' It is not only something which we enter, but something which we receive. That life of love that is the kingdom is an atmosphere. It is like the glorious air we breathe; it must be both about us and within us or we die. And we cannot receive it into us, any more than we can enter into it, until all the useless dirt has been scoured out of our souls and they are pure and receptive as the souls of little children.

*God So Loved the World*

## SIMPLICITY

Those poor and simple men, the shepherds, were in their humility so near to God that they could actually perceive

47

the angel and accept his message as the truth without a shadow of doubt in their minds. And their journey to their Saviour was a very short one. But the journey is not so easy for clever men. For them Gabriel is not the child's angel of intuition, near and swift and warm, but the angel of reason, cold and distant like a star in the sky. Long and difficult thought brings them to their Saviour, and the way can be hard and may take years.

*God So Loved the World*


## HUMILITY

One thinks, I was so sure of my own decency, yet I could do this thing. I thought myself so safely grounded in fidelity, or whatever the particular virtue may be upon which one prides oneself, that no temptation could shake me, yet I went down like a rootless tree. The shock shatters one's self-complacency, and that, I suppose, gives the light its chance.

*The Heart of the Family*


## REVERENCE

When you have learned truly to reverence . . . you seek no further. When you can worship the divinity of life in the rustle of a leaf or the curve of a baby's cheek there is no point in ambition. You have already attained to all that there is.

*Green Dolphin Country*

# TRUST

## *The Feeding of the Five Thousand*

In the crowd of people leaving their homes and following Our Lord out into the wilderness we see a picture of the way in which he looks after us if we follow him. They had no food with them and it looked as though the feeble among them would be faint with hunger before the day was over; and many of the sick folk, dragging along in the broiling sun, must have wondered if they would survive; yet at the end of the day, all was well with them.

*God So Loved the World*

## OBEDIENCE

Jean Anderson . . . had always done what she had to do and faced what she had to face. If many of her fears and burdens would have seemed unreal to another woman there was nothing unreal about her courage . . .

This morning, for instance, putting on her outdoor shoes in her bedroom to call on the new Miss Lindsay, terror had come upon her. The dread of meeting someone who did not know about her was one of her worst fears. They would try and talk to her, and she would not know what they were talking about, or if she did know, and she knew more often than people realized, and the answers were lucid in her mind, she would not be able to find the words to give them form. She would see the surprise in the face of the newcomer, the embarrassment, and then the relief with which he effected his escape . . . She had fumbled helplessly with the knotted laces of her shoes and got in a panic because she could not tie them. Because of course she had known she must go. She always did the thing because in obedience lay the integrity that God asked of her. If anyone had asked her what she meant by integrity she would not have

49

been able to tell them, but she had seen it once like a picture in her mind, a root going down into the earth and drinking deeply there. No one was really alive without that root. And meanwhile she had not been able to get her shoes laced. She had stopped struggling, her hands sticky with fear and anxiety, and taking her shoes right off had turned back with blind trust to the beginning again, to the beginning of the action of obedience that always had a wholesome sweetness in it, though it was hard, a foretaste of the end with its humble thankfulness. And then, just as she had bent to pick up her left shoe, it had happened, and she had sat with the shoe in her hand and laughed. Just the sense of her own ridiculous predicament, only she had not been laughing alone. He had laughed with her. After that the knots had come out of the laces quite easily, she had put on her hat and gone. The fear had gone with her, of course, but it had become bearable.

*The Scent of Water*

Strait is the gate and narrow is the way that leads to the kingdom of heaven. The path is narrow as the needle's eye, the kind of little path that children love, the gate small and easy for them to unlatch, the lintel above it adjusted to the height of a child. The path is too narrow for covetous men burdened with possessions, the gate so small that the self-engrossed walk past it without even noticing it, the lintel so low that no proud head can bend itself low enough to get underneath. Worldly growth is an expanding process, a building up and a swelling out, but the paradox of spiritual growth is a refining process; we have to shed one layer of useless and grubby accretion after another until there is nothing left at all but the golden kernel of a child's humble, loving and contrite heart.

*God So Loved the World*

# A HUMBLE HEART

## *Miss Wentworth*

In the pride of life you stood with your hands full of roses, but in old age the petals turned to dust; and then even the dust fell away through your fingers, leaving you with nothing but your empty hands, stained with dirt . . . Just your sin, that was all you seemed to have at the end . . .

Her empty dirty hands . . . She sat bemusedly looking at them and slowly her misery turned to a faint glow of inward joy as she began to wonder if perhaps they had more value than all she had possessed. Empty, they could be cleansed. She was humble now, she had nothing and could be cleansed. It might be true that . . . loss . . . was the one thing needful.

*The Rosemary Tree*

# A LOVING HEART

To love God in the beauty of holiness . . . is the one thing supremely worth doing, and the life that gives us the chance of trying to do it is, whatever its suffering, most precious to us.

*God So Loved the World*

If love of God comes first with you, then you deny yourself to keep His commandments, you give away your whole life to Him and glory in what the world calls loss.

*The Rosemary Tree*

# A CONTRITE HEART

*Parson Hawthyn*

His memory sometimes failed now in his old age. Ah, that was the hardest thing to relinquish! Vigour of mind. The material things were not hard to give up, but memory, intellect, even perhaps at last the power to pray . . . from these it would be hard to part. Being human, he was feeling slightly sorry for himself at the moment and he found himself praying that he might never part from them, that he might die before that final stripping. Then . . . he remembered the season. Christmas Eve. The Child in the manger had not only stripped Himself of the glory of heaven, but of His wisdom too. The doing of the will of God had caused Him to lie there possessing neither memory, intellect nor the power to pray. Parson Hawthyn was ashamed . . .

*The White Witch*

Shall I not see that to live is to have relinquished
beauty to the sequestration of the dark,
and yet that the spirit of man, benighted, vanquished,
has folded wings, and shall use them as the lark
into the sun beyond the cold clouds flinging
her desperate hope, not reaching where she has striven
but soaring for ever beyond herself, and singing
high above earth as she is low in heaven?

*The Uncelestial City*, Humbert Wolfe

It made him feel cold with apprehension . . . 'To live is to have relinquished beauty to the sequestration of the dark.' Was that what life must be, a continual loss of beauty? Youth, love, happiness, health, work, life itself, one left them one by one behind as one went on. 'Relinquish.' It was a good word. It suggested not the tearing away of treasures but the willing and graceful sacrifice of them . . .

He turned . . . to rejoice in that picture of the soul as a bird-like thing, winged and free even when the evil humours and the despair of a man seemed to himself to keep him earthbound . . . 'Fly away and be at rest.' At last the mounting lark ascended so high into the light that she was lost in it and was not seen again.

*The Bird in the Tree*

On earth the great days cannot, and may not, endure. 'This is too good to last,' we say, and at our happiest we are often most afraid. When a great man is at the height of his power then it is slipping from him. When physical beauty has come to the peak of perfection decay has set in. The mystery of spiritual survival, not only of the souls of men but of anything that in its earthly flowering has caught some reflection of the shining of God, is something we must believe in if we believe in God at all, since all beauty is a part of Him, but is as much beyond our comprehension as He is Himself. We only know that relinquishment is one of the laws of our being, and that we must submit to it, since it is our only pathway back to God. We journey out from Him gathering to us one after another of His gracious gifts, and we journey home putting them back one by one into His hands. It should not be so difficult for us, for we know where they are.

*Saint Francis of Assisi*

# 5

# Suffering

'If anyone wants to come with me, he must
forget self, take up his cross . . . and follow me.'
*Luke 9:23*

## THE PROBLEM OF SUFFERING

In this world where we live now no single man or woman
can come to the end of their life without suffering, some
not more than can reasonably be borne, some more than
that, some intolerably and hideously. If we all suffered
equally there would be no problem, but we do not suffer
equally, and it is the inequality that creates the heart-
searching for those among us who believe in the love of
God. My father would say austerely, 'It does not matter
what we suffer as long as we suffer enough.' He believed
whole-heartedly in the cleansing and redemptive power of
pain and its value when offered as intercession, but he
acknowledged the problem and staggered under it because
of the fact that unbearable suffering can corrupt as well as
redeem.

'I am tormented by the suffering of so many good and
innocent people,' someone said to Archbishop Temple
during the last war. 'Yes,' he replied, 'but what bothers me
even more is the suffering of the wicked.'

That would suggest that how an individual takes his

pain, what he allows it to do in him and through him, is much more important than the pain itself. The scene of suffering in each person seems to be a battleground where a thing evil in its origin comes up against the battling love of God that would transform it into an instrument of victory; not victory for the individual alone but also for God himself in the cosmic battle between good and evil . . .

But the deepest mystery of all, for me, is this one. Suffering, we believe, stems from evil, and evil has no part in the will of God. Yet God allowed the cruelty, jealousy and cowardice of man to put his son upon the cross and when he was there made no move to end his torture; God himself in man had to stick it out until the end. And so God and the suffering caused by sin are inseparably united, and will be so until sin ends. The mind boggles but there is enormous comfort here. For one thing it is hard to doubt the love of a God who is ready to suffer and die for us. For another thing, when we suffer we must be as close to God as we are to the pain. At the worst of it we may feel, as Christ did, that God forsakes when unbearable pain takes over. But the truth must be the reverse. Devout people used to say of pain or grief, 'God touched me.' Gerard Manley Hopkins says, 'And dost thou touch me afresh? Over again I feel thy finger and find thee.'

*The Joy of the Snow*


## FINDING GOD IN OUR PAIN

Man . . . To him it had been given to pass through life and death to life again, and know them one; to rise to the very peak and height of agony and find himself looking into the eyes of God beneath the crown of thorns, to fall through the bottomless abyss and find himself kneeling at the feet of God pierced through with nails, to probe each way through doubting and despair and find the arms of God outstretched in love upon the cross.

*The Castle on the Hill*

# FINDING ONENESS IN SUFFERING

Though personal suffering can seem to a man an entirely lonely and isolating thing, a prison within a prison, it is in actual fact the exact opposite. Through it he reaches the only real unity, oneness with the whole of suffering creation.

*The Heart of the Family*

## AWARENESS OF A SUFFERING WORLD

After the little succession of family disasters I fell headlong into what is called a nervous breakdown, a state which as all its victims know can be terrifying . . .

Blind as a bat I could not see that what I had to put up with myself was not only a microscopic burden but also an extremely common one, and I scarcely considered the example of my father, carrying his recurrent darkness so selflessly that it damaged neither mind nor body. I had hardly considered anyone but myself until the day I went to the oculist . . .

I sat [in the waiting room] . . . mounded up with self-pity and glooming over my fate, until I found myself looking across at the stranger opposite me, an elderly woman sitting upright and completely still. Her face had the glazed look of someone who has suffered much, something that I did not recognise then, but I do now. She was very near me and I could look directly into her eyes. She did not look as though she were blind but her eyes did not see me. It is a strange experience to look straight into the eyes of someone who is not even aware that you are there. I began to feel shivery. What she feared, what she had already endured, I could not know, but I did know that anything I had suffered myself faded into nothingness in comparison. For a few moments I seemed to fall into a cold misery that I cannot describe. It was not her alone, it was all the people

56

whom until now . . . I had refused to think about; battening them down under hatches so that I should not have to feel too miserable. Quite suddenly, if only for a short while, she had let me through into their company.

*The Joy of the Snow*


The deeper you go into pain the more certain you are that all that happens to you has an explanation and a purpose.

*Towers in the Mist*


## STRENGTH IN ADVERSITY

All times of devastation . . . leave the survivors with a feeling of amazement. Is it possible that such weak creatures as we know ourselves to be have coped with this? Done what had to be done, borne what had to be borne, picked up the pieces and become ready to begin again and go on living . . .

No one supposes that this competence and survival has much to do with their everyday selves. Christians acknowledge the power and grace of God and marvel at it. Non-believers marvel at the discovery of a toughness within them that they did not know they had, a source of strength that seems not available in everyday living and opens up only when disaster strikes. The believer acknowledges this too but gives the name of God to the well of power within him, and believes also that he has a prepared path under his feet and moves along it step by step to a prepared end. Much later, looking back, he realises how many stars there were showing the way at the cross-roads, stars which can be called either coincidence or Providence according to personal belief.

*The Joy of the Snow*

Endurance was never for nothing. Something enduring came out of it, or it was not endurance. If it took you nowhere, then it was just nonsense, and he had clung to it for too long for him to think it that. The life-line to which the wrecked sailor clings in a raging sea is not nonsense, but, for him, the most important fact of existence, and it would not be there at all if it were not held firmly upon some shore that through the blinding spume he cannot see. The problem for him is simply that of holding on.

*The Heart of the Family*


## FEAR OF SUFFERING

All we are asked to bear we can bear. That is a law of the spiritual life. The only hindrance to the working of this law, as of all benign laws, is fear.

*The Child from the Sea*


## COPING WITH FEAR

Show no sign of your fear, offer it to God . . . and the costly gift will be a more acceptable prayer than any repetition of mere words.

\*   \*   \*

Be willing to be afraid, don't be afraid of your fear.

\*   \*   \*

Don't fight it, accept it without shame, just as you would accept any other limitation you happen to be born with . . . Willing acceptance is half the battle.

*Gentian Hill*


## THE NEED FOR ACCEPTANCE

There is always the Thing . . . the hidden Thing, some fear or pain or shame, temptation or bit of self-knowledge that you can never explain to another ... For it is the essence of it that it is, humanly speaking, a lonely thing ... If you just endure it simply because you must, like a boil on the neck, or fret yourself to pieces trying to get rid of it, or cadge sympathy for it, then it can break you. But if you accept it as a secret burden borne secretly for the love of Christ, it can become your hidden treasure. For it is your point of contact with Him, your point of contact with that fountain of refreshment down at the roots of things. 'Oh Lord, thou fountain of living waters ...' In those deep green pastures where cool waters are there is no separation. Our point of contact with the suffering Christ is our point of contact with every other suffering man and woman, and is the source of our life.

*The Heart of the Family*

## LEARNING TO ACCEPT

I remember now that I did accept, that night when I woke up in the hospital room ... and I realized that I was sane again. I was so thankful that I said, yes, I'll do it. You might say that wasn't a real acceptance because what I'd refused had already happened to me. But yet it was. You can go on refusing even after it's happened to you, like the child who screams and kicks the door after it's been shut up in the dark room. Or you can sit quietly down in the dark and watch for the return of light.

*The Scent of Water*

## COMING TO TERMS WITH SUFFERING

He remembered ... as he looked at the squares of moonlight lying on the floor, the time when he had first realized that pain is a thing that we must face and come to terms with if life is to be lived with dignity and not merely muddled through like an evil dream.

It had been when his father was dying. His mother had not troubled over much to keep him out of sight and sound of his father's pain; she had thought he was too little to understand. But he had understood. He had been old for his age and already sensitivized by more than his normal share of those terrors of childhood of which no child will ever speak; the horror of a creeping shadow on a wall, the sudden awakening at night to the terrifying dark, the conviction that a nightmare beast is stabled beneath the bed and the strange panting fear awakened by lightning and big bangs; these he had known to the full, and they had seemed to him all summed up in this terrible thing that he had seen, this pain that had gripped his father. Terrified by it he had fled one evening to the dark attic, slammed the door and flung himself down sobbing upon the floor. He had sobbed for an hour, sobbed himself sick and exhausted until at last, childlike, he had forgotten what it was he was crying about and had become instead absorbed in the moonlight on the floor. It had been like a pool of silver, enclosed and divided up into neat squares by the bars of the window. He had counted the squares and the lines, dark and light, and had been delighted with them. He had touched each with his finger, this way and that, and had been utterly comforted . . .

Later, in bed, he had been comforted once more by the thought of that pattern. In some vague way he had understood that dark things are necessary; without them the silver moonlight would just stream away into nothingness, but with them it can be held and arranged into beautiful squares.

*The Bird in the Tree*


## THE MYSTERIOUS ONE-NESS OF JOY AND PAIN

Could you understand the meaning of light if there were no darkness to point the contrast? Day and night, life and death, love and hatred, since none of these things can have any being at all apart from the existence of the other, you can no more separate them than you can separate the two sides of a coin. To possess one is to possess the other . . .

*Green Dolphin Country*

If you believe in God omnipresent then you must believe that everything that comes into your life, person or event, must have something of God in it to be experienced and loved; not hated.

*Green Dolphin Country*

## MISS GILES

'I've never welcomed anything difficult or painful. I've always resented it and hit back. I can see now that to have welcomed the slings and arrows might have been to welcome love.'

*   *   *

Why should one evade suffering? Evasion was denial of truth. 'Brother Fire, God made you beautiful and strong and useful; I pray you be courteous with me,' Saint Francis had said when the man came to cauterize his eyes. One could ask a brother to be courteous but one could not deny his brotherhood. To turn aside from one brother was to turn aside from all the brethren, from birds and beasts and flowers and children, from verse and music. One could not pick and choose. It had to be all or nothing.

*The Rosemary Tree*

*There are those who suffer greatly, and yet, through the recognition that pain can be a thread in the pattern of God's weaving, find the way to a fundamental joy.*

*A Book of Faith*

Capricious fortune took it into her head sometimes to lay upon a wound a salve of such value that a man became positively glad of the wound . . . But no, he did not believe in capricious fortune but in a carefully woven pattern where every tightly stretched warp thread of pain laid the foundation for a woof thread of joy.

*Gentian Hill*

Spring . . . always returns . . . However terrible life may seem at a given moment darkness always passes. Spring is the smile of God and his joy is entwined in the roots of our existence and cannot be destroyed. No night is without its hour of total darkness and no human soul escapes moments of total despair, but spring comes back and the God-centred soul is tough enough to cling to the knowledge and utterly refuse to let it go.

*The Child from the Sea*

# Part III

# *I am the Truth*

'Set your troubled hearts at rest.
Believe in God and believe also
in me.'

*John 14:1*

The word 'Believe' rings through all [Our Lord's] work of healing. He could only heal where there was belief in his power to heal. 'Be not afraid, only believe,' he would say, and when the answer was, 'Lord, I believe! Help thou mine unbelief,' then he could answer, 'Thy faith hath saved thee; go in peace.' Faith was, and is, the door from pain to peace, from death to life, both for the body and for the soul.

*God So Loved the World*

It may be difficult, in the face of the problem of human suffering, to believe in God . . . but if you destroy God you do not solve your problem but merely leave yourself alone with it.

*A City of Bells*

## PAIN AND THE LOVE OF GOD

My mother's illness had troubled me all my life, and I felt guilty as well as unhappy, so bound together are we all by the guilt and sorrow of the world that we all share. But I confess with shame that I do not believe my faith in the love of God was badly shaken until the evil touched me myself . . . When my mother suffered I was miserable and my faith in God's love was sorely tried. When I suffered myself it was nearly shattered . . .

I could not totally disbelieve in God because during my worst and most despairing nights there had seemed to be something there; some rock down at the bottom . . . And always my parents' love and faith, the world's beauty and the sound of great music, seemed unexplainable without God . . . Therefore I had to find a God I could love. I could not love a God who did not stop this suffering therefore I had to have a God who could not, a God who was not Almighty. I was aware of the cosmic struggle since I had experienced the faint echo of it in myself, the spiritual powers of good and evil in conflict. I worked it out that one was not stronger than the other, and at the end of it all evil might win. God might again die and this time have no resurrection. But if he was finally defeated it would be our fault, not his, for he would have withstood evil to the utmost limit, as he did on Calvary, and would die only because we are afraid to do the same. Our wounds are in his flesh, always, our griefs in his heart, but he is powerless to stop the evil of sin and pain by himself. He is a God who needs us and cannot do without us. I could love that weak God.

I was happy with this for a while, and then I told my father of my conclusions. The result was disastrous. How unoriginal human beings are! Our great ideas are seldom new. I had thought up the heresy of Manicheism, a faith for which men and women had been willing to be martyred, and which had tempted even Augustine. It was hard to let go of my lovely heresy, but my father had no mercy on it. A God who is not Almighty is not God, and to believe in his possible defeat is not comforting; that way lies despair.

I do not remember all he said of his own faith, possibly I did not understand it, but I remember my own conclusions. If our own small intuition, upheld by the experience of the saints and mystics of all religions through all the centuries, persists in murmuring that God exists then there is nothing left for us except the humble acceptance of paradox and mystery. If it is true that God is Almighty, it is also true that he needs us, since he chose that his son should be true man as well as true God, by this choice making Christ and man inseparable. Apart from Christ we have no life; we are merely a dead leaf fallen from the tree. Apart from us he has no body in the world, no hands and feet and heart and voice to bring God's mercy to a suffering world.

*The Joy of the Snow*

## THE BEGINNINGS OF FAITH

Children lucky enough to grow up in a Christian home are given a good start, since small children are copy-cats and believe what their parents believe and do as their parents do, and later they sail out from a harbour that has a lighthouse on the rocks and however far they travel it is difficult to forget the harbour with the green fields of childhood behind it, and the light always haunts them; it is a finger of light feeling for them.

But neither a copy-cat religion nor a haunting is faith. Somewhere, if one is lucky enough to have faith, however wobbly and constantly tested it may be, there must have been a moment of conviction that fell like a seed to the earth and struck root.

*The Joy of the Snow*

What *was* faith? Was that easy, happy belief of the old days, that had added so much to the pleasure of life, perhaps not faith at all? He wondered if he was now, for the first time in his life, actually experiencing faith. This fight with no certainty that there was anything to fight for, this going out into the night with no belief that the dawn would ever come, was it perhaps the real thing of which the other, easier thing had been only a fore-taste . . . ? He felt certain that it was so. Yet of what use was this faith, either to himself or to the world . . . ? Not to know its use was the very essence of it. Faith was a charge in the dark by blindfold men, urged on by instinct only. Of

67

that instinct one knew nothing except that it was the greatest thing in life.

## FINDING FAITH IN JOY

She turned from the shimmering sea to look at the golden gorse and the regal foxgloves spiring up against the sky. Far up a lark sang, crazy with ecstasy, and, wonder of wonders, on a thistle nearby was a goldfinch singing his squeaky little song . . . How she loved these things! Each scrap and shred of beauty was a feather in wings that bore her soaring up and up towards the lark at heaven's gate. Keats began singing in her mind again.

> Feel we these things? – that moment have we
> passed into a sort of oneness, and our state
> Is like a floating spirit's.

*Island Magic*

## FINDING FAITH IN DARKNESS

She had never before been quite alone in the Cathedral . . . and it was dark. Vast curtains of shadow fell from the invisible roof . . . And high up in the darkness that her sight could not penetrate he was there upon the rood . . . the man on the rood, sharing the same darkness with her and with a vast multitude of people whom she seemed to know and love. How much more friendly it is when you cannot see, thought Miss Montague, and how much closer we are to him. Why should we always want a light? He chose darkness for us, darkness of the womb and of the stable, darkness in the garden, darkness on the cross and in the grave. Why do I demand certainty? That is not faith.

Why do I want to understand? How can I understand this great web of sin and ugliness and love and suffering and joy and life and death when I don't understand the little tangle of good and evil that is myself? I've enough to understand. I understand that he gave me light that I might turn to him . . . He shared his light with me that I, turned, might share with him the darkness of his redemption. Why did I despair? What do I want? If it is him I want he is here, not only love in light illuming all that he has made but love in darkness dying for it.

*The Dean's Watch*

## THE SEARCH FOR GOD

The beseeching . . . the crying out, like the upthrust of the green shoot from the sod, or the leap of the flame from the charred wood. So long as that cry goes up from a soul, though it be for she knows not what, she is not lost . . . Each fresh leap of the flame from the charred wood lights your footsteps a little farther through the dark.

*The Herb of Grace*

## DIFFERING FAITHS

He believed that truth is a great globe and that men see only that part of it upon which for them the light shines. He believed that through any creed held in sincerity the finger of God can reach and touch a man. He believed that if men struggled to find the light, they would reach the light, not only in spite of but through their mistakes and limitations. But there was one way in which they would not find it, and that was by turning back on the path upon which for them the light shone and taking another man's path for the sake of expediency or peace. He recalled the words of Sir Thomas More. 'I never intend (God being my good lord) to pin my soul at another man's back, not even the best man that I know.'

*The White Witch*

O Lord, grant wisdom and kindness, and that respect for a differing faith that you asked of us with your command that we should love our enemies.

*A Diary of Prayer*

Faith is a gift that we cannot compel, and it seems to be given more to the measure of our loving than to the struggling of our minds. It can strike suddenly, or come as slowly as the greening of spring.

Whether at once, as once at a crash Paul,
Or as Austin, a lingering-out sweet skill,

and the skill is Christ's, and cannot be described, only worshipped and adored. There are those who can believe in the love of God without believing that Christ on the cross is God. In the face of human misery that is a leap of faith that I should find it hard to take. The love of God is too mighty and dreadful for our contemplation but in accepting the life and death of Christ as the utmost revelation we can have of it now, in this world and this time, I can feel at rest. Does it seem impossible, too startling to be true, that a man on the gallows should be God? Yet in this amazing universe where every new discovery shocks us afresh, is it not just what we should expect of this startling Creator? As the years go on we fall in love with him more and more, we cannot help it. The mind may reel and protest but we cannot help it. His immense love is too strong. Our frail loving is too strong. Finally we fight against neither. I do not know certainly who it was, though I think it was Charles Williams,

70

who when he was finally captured said, 'there is nothing
possible for me now except to believe the impossible.'

*The Joy of the Snow*


## FAITH, HOPE AND LOVE

Of the three cardinal virtues faith comes first, as though
it were the most important, and yet they are so inter-
twined that one can hardly put one before the other. What
priest at his ordination, or bride and bridegroom at their
wedding, would dare to stand before God and make their
promises of faithfulness if they did not have a firm hope
that their love was strong enough to keep them? And once
the love of God has been revealed to us in his son, and we
set out on the prodigal's journey back to the Father, we
could never keep going if we did not believe that Christ
walks with us all the way, and hope for the heaven of
union with him at the end of it all.

And so it is hard to separate faith from hope and love
and try to look at it by itself. Doubt, too, would seem to be a
part of faith. Loving the light so much, could we face night
without our confident hope that the sun will rise in the
morning? But what guarantee have we got that it will?
None, really. And on some nights that we can all of us
remember, nights of the soul that can last for months or
years as well as winter nights of grief or illness, we doubt if
it will. But time does drag by and the dawn comes, and we
find that faith given back to us after a night of doubt is a
stronger thing, and far more valuable to us than faith that
has never been tested. The loss, grief, and pain we experienced now seem a part of faith because they taught us to
trust God, and we now have a deeper joy and peace in
believing. Yet all that is truly good, all that comes from
God, has its own simplicity that belongs to itself alone.
What is the essence of faith, the thing breathed out from
the heart of the simplicity?

71

. . . Since sinful human beings are far too complicated to understand simplicity, of course, we cannot know, but could it perhaps be likened to a scent? The scent of the white hart who leaps away into the forest with a speed that makes the hunter's pursuit hopeless? Or of a flower, an elusive scent that comes on the wind and is gone again before the child in the garden can tell from which direction it drifted. Or we could say it is like music heard by a man who has lost his way in the dark; the echo of a bell or of a voice singing. He does not know where it comes from, but it speaks to him of life and companionship.

Saint Paul says, 'Faith is the substance of things hoped for, the evidence of things not seen.' The faith he speaks of came to him after he had himself been hunted down and captured on the Damascus road. For this hunt, it would seem, is a two-way thing. There is no knowing when the white hart will change direction, as terrifying in his backward leap as an arc of white lightning; or as gentle as the unicorn in Rilke's poem. 'Whitely it stole up to a maid — to *be* within the silver mirror and in her.' But in spite of his gentleness, she was not able to see the creature. All she knew of him was the fleeting reflection in the mirror and the sense of inward possession, and all Saint Paul had of the lightning was physical blindness and the pulsing warmth invading the pit of his empty heart. But when his sight came back, the sky and the trees, and the white roads winding over the hills, must have smiled at him with a beauty as strange and new as the knowledge that his heart seemed now to be beating for the first time. He was reborn into a new life for he had received the gift of faith, and it was for him so tremendous a gift that he could use the words 'substance' and 'evidence' when speaking of something both untouchable and invisible.

We live in a maze of symbols, all of them from the sun to a bird's feather, from the Bach B minor Mass down to the echo of a bell, uniting to give us this multi-coloured treasure that starts us off on the journey that has been described down the centuries in so many myths and

72

stories, but is always the same journey. The prodigal son and the Magi were journeying to the same place and Person; they were hunters on the same trail. The prodigal son caught the scent of some remembered goodness, the fragrance of some garden at life's beginning and of Someone who had walked with him there. Or so, on his good days, the song of the birds and the colours of the wayside flowers seemed to tell him . . . On his bad days he could not smell a thing; except the stink of his own dirt . . . But he went on, sometimes with the faint sound of water in his ears from far-off streams. How could he know that at the other end of the trail another hunter was running out to meet him? And how could the Magi know either in those times of darkness and confusion that when their star blinked and went out, and they floundered off the road, they would ever get on it again? It was only when the stable door opened and the light came down the path to meet them that they knew their journey had not been hopeless.

The author of the Epiphany collect must have been much like Saint Paul, for he speaks with the same shattering confidence. 'Mercifully grant that we, which know thee now by faith, may after this life have the fruition of thy glorious Godhead.' The fruition, the completeness of the Godhead. What a thing to dare to hope for! It sounds ridiculous, yet both men, and an amazing number of saints and mystics both before and after them, have said the same thing . . . We exhausted, futile travellers, losing the way, falling in the dark, struggling on again, will ultimately get there . . . It is an immense hope and is the gift of faith; and faith, it seems, is in part a readiness to receive the symbols not only as gifts of immeasurable value in themselves but as far more; echoes, gleams, reflections, intimations of what George Macdonald calls 'the secret too great to be told'. The symbols cannot tell us what it is, but if we are ready and willing to watch and listen and receive, they breathe out to us the knowledge that it is *there*. To breathe in this breath, to catch its perfume or the echo of its music, is to experience the faith that Christ likened to a grain of mustard seed, a simple thing, yet hiding within itself the possibility of miraculous transformation. What the essence of our faith can be, I still do not really know, but I do know the words that come to me when I hear great music or see the sun lighting up the spiders' webs on a morning when the garden is spangled with dew. 'I bring you good tidings of great joy.'

*A Book of Faith*

# Part IV

# *I am Life*

'Because I live, you too will live;
then you will know that I am in
   my Father,
and you in me and I in you.'
*John 14:19–20*

# THE LIFE-LINE

As the great trees of the primeval forest closed about him . . . the earth his mother for the first time held out her arms and pulled him close. As with his spirit in the deeps of prayer so now with his body in her arms, separateness vanished. The same ecstatic life that pulsed in his body throbbed also in the body of his horse, blazed in the sunlight, chimed in the birdsong all about him, sang in the wind in the treetops, aspired in the delicate veining of leaves and grasses and the silent miraculous unfolding of the flowers. He was in them and they in him . . .

In that moment he saw everything about him, every frond of green fern and every shaft of sunlight, as a voyager from the eternal creating Spirit, yet not parted from that Spirit because the life within it was as it were a thread of divinity, a gossamer life-line from Creator to creature that nothing in heaven or earth could ever break. Through whatever changes the creature might pass, changes to which man in his ignorance might give the name of death, the life-line still held and brought it back at last to the Creator's heart.

*Green Dolphin Country*

# THE PERFECT CIRCLE OF LIFE

The dying often seem to feel themselves back again at their starting point, reliving the days of their youth and remembering the things that they thought they had forgotten. They are no longer the old man or woman only but the whole person, all that they have been and done gathered into a unity to face the end that is also the beginning.

*Saint Francis of Assisi*

One's life is a complete, rounded, timeless thing rooted in eternity . . . what we once had is ours forever . . . what we will have is already present with us . . . at no time in our lives are we ever anything but immeasurably and inconceivably rich and blessed.

*Green Dolphin Country*

Do you imagine that past happiness is lost? You will come round to it again when the circle is complete, and at the end of it all nothing will be eternally lost except evil.

*The Heart of the Family*

## THE FREEDOM OF DEATH

All I wanted was that the thinning walls of my bodily life should let me go, cast me out like a captive lark freed and flung from a window. And I thought, this is death, and it seemed that I sang already.

*The Scent of Water*

## THE FEAR OF DEATH

The dark auditorium with its unseen crowd of witnesses is a frightening thing, pressing in upon our poor little garish stage, frightening because we know nothing of it.

Yet when our play is ended and the house lights go up we shall see many kindly faces. It is a house, remember, a friendly place. There is a prayer by the great Dean John Donne that I often repeat to myself. 'Bring us, O Lord God, at our last awakening, into the house and gate of heaven, to enter into that gate and dwell in that house where there shall be no darkness or dazzling, but one equal light; no noise nor silence, but one equal music; no fears nor hopes, but one equal possession; no ends nor beginnings, but one equal eternity; in the habitations of Thy glory and dominion, world without end!'

*The Dean's Watch*


## LUCILLA'S DREAM OF HEAVEN

She was walking through a forest in a strange country. About her the great trees soared upwards, stretching their branches against the sky like arms held up in adoration. They were like living creatures, those trees, and so were the myriad flowers that grew about her feet. In their colour and scent they were as an army that praised God; the ground was singing bright with them. There were carolling birds in the trees who did not fly away when she came near them, and little brown furry beasts in the undergrowth who had never known the meaning of fear. There was water not far away. She could hear the murmur of it and see the calm blue of it shining through the trees. And yet behind this music there was a deep quiet. Though she moved onwards yet she was resting. The music and the silence, the movement and the rest, seemed co-existent together. She felt happy with a quite indescribable happiness that was yet best described by the word cleanliness. In body, mind and spirit she felt clean, with her thoughts unmuddied and her body a perfect instrument of the spirit within her that she could feel was as a polished mirror to reflect and transmit the light about her.

79

That light, too, was indescribable. It was something like the light of earthly dawn that she had seen before she slept, holding the same depth of colour, the same coolness and warmth as the light of the sun and moon shining together, yet it transcended that as greatly as the light of the sun transcends the flicker of a candle. The music that was all about her, lovely yet diffuse as light, seemed to gather itself into one single phrase, as when the voice of a solo singer soars above the harmony of orchestra and voices, and she heard the words of it. 'They have no need of the sun, neither of the moon, to shine in it, for the Lord God giveth them light.'

Then she laughed out of her joy, for she knew where she was. And she knew too why she was here, and why she had been born into that life that she had left, and why those whom she loved had been born into it, had suffered in it and had left it; to reflect and transmit this light from the mirror of a pain-cleansed spirit . . .

As she became more familiar with this country she knew that as she went on the boundaries of it would widen. It was the glorified beauty of the familiar and habitable earth that she saw now, the trees and flowers and creatures that made up the sweetness of it, but soon she would see more. She would see the spirits of those she loved going about the purposes of God bathed in the light of his perpetual compassion; and at the last she would see even farther; but of that she dared not yet think . . . Yet, thinking of it, she began to run, effortlessly, almost as though she were winged . . .

*The Bird in the Tree*


## JUDGMENT

What do we all feel, at the end of our work? Near the end perhaps, of our life? Much the same, I expect. If like myself we are one of the lucky ones, overwhelming gratitude. And mixed with the gratitude, shame; for living and working should all be done in obedience to whatever vision of God may have been given to us; and how we do fail our vision of him.

What do I believe about the vision of God, and about judgment? Our ancestors believed that all souls would stand before the judgment seat of God, and that many would be sent to a hell of lasting torment. Today our ideas are less concrete but more merciful. What do I believe myself about judgment? My own picture of these things is clear in my mind. It is only my own picture but I expect I share it with many others. With me it is, literally, a picture, for even in old age I cannot manage to grow up sufficiently either to listen to music, to think or pray without seeing pictures in my mind.

I believe that we are created by love and that sooner or later the persuasion of love will draw us up out of our darkness to stand in its exquisite light and see ourselves at last as we really are. The picture I see is of a seed deep in the earth. Somewhere, far up above the weight of darkness pressing upon the pitiful little seed, is the drawing and the calling of the sun. It seems an impossible journey towards something that has never been seen and cannot be known, but half unconsciously the blind seed puts out roots to steady itself, pushes an imploring hand upwards and starts the struggle. The poor mad poet Christopher Smart said, 'the flower glorifies God and the root parries the adversary.' The struggling plant knows as little about the flower he will presently be as he knows about the God he will glorify, but the flower calls to him too as he pushes up through thick darkness with the adversary clinging to his feet.

The picture of the soul now turns in my mind from that of a plant to a little animal, like a mole, scrabbling with his forepaws to make an upward tunnel, kicking out with his hindlegs at the adversary who tries ceaselessly to drag him back and down. Often he *is* dragged down, but he

81

recovers himself and goes on and with each fresh beginning he is a little higher up; and always the pull of the sun is far more powerful than that of the adversary.

He is through at last and stands in the sun, and sometimes in my picture he is a little animal with trembling paws covering his face, and sometimes he is a shivering spike of a flower with a closed bud. The sun must woo the opened eyes to peep between the chinks of the paws, or persuade the closed petals to open a little way. It is enough. A little warmth, a little light, and the creature can know for whom, and for what he was made. For love, that he may love perfectly, and perfected be useful to the love that has loved him from the beginning and will love him to the end.

But meanwhile, what is he? It is the judgment. There is no judgment seat for the sun does not judge him; merely warms him and gives him light. He is his own judge and strengthened by the warmth he looks at himself in the light. What has he made of himself in the dark tunnel? What is he like? A dirty little animal. A shaky bit of stalk holding up a crumpled bud that has no beauty in it. The knowledge is agony, for with blind eyes down in the dark he had thought a good deal of himself, and the agony is both his judgment and his inspiration. He cannot stand in the light like this. The paws go out in supplication in my picture, or the petals push away the calyx and take on the shape of praying hands. Do what you like with me. Whatever the cost, wash me and make me clean that I may be with you.

*The Joy of the Snow*


## HELL

If one believes in a God of love what can one think about hell? To my sorrow I am not a thinker. Thinking, with me, is not much more than a sort of confused worrying, but trying to sort out one's confusion is a great help to worriers, even if it is not thought.

As reported in the gospels Christ said some frightening things about hell and I have spent miserable moments with them, for I was taught that we must not pick out from the teaching of Christ the things we happen to like and repudiate the rest. But I cannot see that anywhere in what are called 'the hard sayings' Christ says that any human soul will live eternally in hell. His chosen word to describe hell is 'fire'. Fire purifies and fire destroys, but never preserves a living thing plunged into it alive in an eternal unchanging state. So there would seem to be two fires, the purification fire in which a thing may be held for a time that it may be purged and annealed, and the fire that destroys utterly.

I believe that in the parable of Dives and Lazarus, Dives is in purgatorial fire, for in his concern for his family one can see the beginning of the death of self-love. But in the parable of the sheep and the goats it appears that the latter have finally rejected love, for they hear dreadful words, 'Depart from me, ye wicked, into everlasting fire.' This surely does not mean the eternal torment of a soul in the eternal fire but its destruction. This, Christ thinks, is fearful enough, since Saint Matthew's gospel reports him as saying, 'Fear him who is able to destroy both soul and body in hell.' And indeed it is fearful that any soul that God made for total love should be totally destroyed, but I cannot think that the destruction contradicts those greatest of all words, 'I, if I be lifted up, will draw all men unto me.' That sentence almost gives the definition of a man; a creature still capable of wrenching his eyes off himself and looking up, a creature (unknown to himself, perhaps) secretly longing for love and capable of it. If there should ever be a creature who had lost even the capability he would be no longer a man but a devil.

Christ said, 'Everlasting fire.' What did he mean by that 'everlasting'? God alone is everlasting, so did he say that the cleansing and destroying fires are God himself? Men have always looked up at the life-giving sun and seen in it a symbol of God, the best they can find to explain their idea of him. 'Thou deckest thyself with light as it were with a garment, and spreadest out the heavens like a curtain,' says the 104th Psalm. 'The earth shall tremble at the look of him; if he do but touch the hills, they shall smoke.' And St Francis says in his *Canticle of the Sun*, 'Fair is he, and he shines with a very great splendour. Oh Lord, he signifies to us, Thee!' So if the two fires are two aspects of God himself, God the Purifier, God the Destroyer, then the hard sayings are hard indeed and divine love must be a terrible thing.

The true lovers of Christ have always thought so and have not shrunk from describing him in his terrible aspect. St John the Divine, describing his vision of Christ, said, 'His countenance was as the Sun shineth in his strength. And when I saw him, I fell at his feet as one dead.' St John the Baptist said, 'Whose fan is in his hand, and he will thoroughly purge his floor, and gather his wheat into the garner; but he will burn up the chaff with unquenchable fire.' Gerard Manley Hopkins enlarges on that saying in one of his sonnets.

. . . O thou terrible, why wouldst thou rude on me
Thy wring-world right foot rock? lay a lionlimb against
  me? scan
With darksome devouring eyes my bruised bones? and
  fan,
O in turns of tempest, me heaped there; me frantic to
  avoid thee and flee?
Why? That my chaff might fly; my grain lie, sheer and
  clear . . .

Christians are sometimes accused of believing in the eternal life of the soul because it is a comforting thought. It makes them feel good because they think their virtue will be rewarded with pie in the sky. But will it? Unless we are saints (which is most unlikely) our scraps of virtue (if any) are no more than filthy rags and what they will be rewarded with is purgatorial fire. It would be much easier to be done with it all at death, not to have to meet the result of what you have done and been but to shelve responsibility and contract right out. It would be much easier but, in the final end, less glorious.

And so having let go of the horror of eternal punishment what do I think about hell now? I believe that in the old sense of the word there is no hell, but that we can use the word in a new way. We can say that all that is contrary to the will of God is dreadful enough to be called hell, in the sense in which most people still use the word. Those who know what it is like to be in such darkness of mind that they feel God has forsaken them think they know what hell is. Those who have been in concentration camps, and have had the whole power of evil concentrated upon them, and those who have endured pain so bad that it is practically beyond human endurance say 'it was hell'. And they are right, since these things are contrary to the will of God and their origin is not in his creative love.

But I believe they are not entirely right for to be imprisoned in evils that are outside his creative love is not to be separated from his redemptive love, since in Christ he experienced these things himself and so left something of love at the heart of each experience. It is possible that he may be found in these things, so often he is, but in any case he is there, and because he is there the eventual end of these agonies is freedom from them.

*The Joy of the Snow*

## THE CHOICE

I would like to believe that no human soul ever becomes a totally evil spirit – a devil – that no human soul is ever destroyed. I want to believe that every single soul reaches God at last. And yet – love cannot compel. Love can draw the little animal up and up, perhaps fighting all the way, to the point where he is aware of the presence of the sun and feels its warmth embrace him. He cries out like Jacob, 'What is your name?' and he knows the answer and what it means. But he has to be asked a question himself. 'Now you know what I am, do you want me?' As it is almost inconceivable to me that love should have to ask such a question of any soul he has created, so it seems equally inconceivable that he would ever receive any answer except, 'Wash me and make me clean that I may be with you.' Yet I have to believe that the soul may refuse if he wishes. And what then? Not eternal torment since the sun is fire, but eternal death ... And yet, Christ conquered death.

One struggles with thoughts and words, and then suddenly they all fall down like the cards with which a child has laboriously tried to build a house, and lie there in chaos at one's feet. For we know nothing. The mystery of the universe and of our tiny breath of being is too great for us. And then one can feel something like the forbidden sin of despair. In this state it comforts me to remember that the great religions of the world have been called 'Traditions of response'. Certainly all true living all down the ages has been a condition of response; to mountains and trees and great waters, to music, poetry, to each other, to loveliness without end, and always it is the response of as much love as we are capable. And as response grows we are capable of more and more and more love. Growth is not sterile. Out beyond all these things must be the reality that speaks through them.

*The Joy of the Snow*


## REDEMPTION

When our own thoughts and words crumble it helps to turn to the mystics who are lifted above our confusions, and to the old myths of the world, some of them almost as old as time.

When I think of what are called 'the last things' and wonder about them I often think of the Hindu myth of redemption. In the story the good and bad spirits alike longed to find the nectar of immortality that is sunk in the ocean of milk, and they made up their minds to churn the ocean in order to find it. They placed a holy mountain in the ocean and began to rotate it, the good people pulling one way and the bad the other, and the first thing they brought up from the depths was the most terrible evil. They were appalled, for the good and bad people alike realised that unless help came it would destroy them all. But help did come for Shiva the Preserver, who is also Shiva the Destroyer, had mercy on them. He took the evil from them and he swallowed it, and pictures of Shiva show him with a blue throat, excoriated by the evil he has taken into his own being. (Christians, reading this story, cannot help remembering the words of Christ, 'This cup which my Father hath given me shall I not drink it?') After that redemption the good and bad people churned again and at last they churned up eternal life. They both had a good look at it, and the good people accepted it and entered into it but the bad people turned away from it and were destroyed.

The myth is like a gold coin with two sides to it. It can be the story of each one of us, filled with horror at the evil we find in the depths of ourselves but powerless to save ourselves from it, or it can be a cosmic story, the story of the universe. In any case it is the same story since love works out from the central point of the soul in ever-widening circles of redemption.

Here is a poem I love, taken from the *Bhagavad-Gita*.

> When goodness grows weak,
> When evil increases,
> I make myself a body.
> In every age I come back
> To deliver the holy,

To destroy the sin of the sinner,
To establish righteousness.

He who knows the nature
Of my task and my holy birth
Is not reborn
When he leaves this body;
He comes to Me.

Flying from fear,
From lust and anger,
He hides in Me,
His refuge and safety.
Burnt clean in the blaze of my being,
In Me many find home.

The Hindu poet, who wrote these verses centuries ago, might have been writing for Christians today, for we would agree with nearly all of it, delighting in the way in which the great religions echo each other as the chimes of the church bells used to do on Christmas night. But for us, though we believe great sons of God walk the world in every age, only one of them is the supreme Son of God who fulfils all longing because he is 'everything God asks of man, and everything man asks of God.'

*The Joy of the Snow*

## Part V

# *Poems*

. . . To search for colours, fumble
   for words,
Strive to catch in earthly song
The echo of greater music,
To fail with heartbreak and give
The heartbreaks to each other
   with our love,
Can this be why we live?

# OUR LADY

Mary, our Mother, how I wish I knew
What you looked like.
Why is it that no one ever told us?
And of your son's likeness we know nothing.
Is silence best?

Who can describe the indescribable
In halting words?
Augustine wrote only of Christ's body,
'He looked us through the lattice of our flesh
And spake us fair.'

The brilliance of eyes on fire with love,
Their piercing glance,
Words of truth, of forgiveness, compassion,
Live in memory and eternity.
The flesh passes.

The body-garment changes with the years.
So strong in youth,
Comely and fair, a joy to look upon,
Then wounds, pain, death, rend the garment and men
Cover the eyes.

Yet still we ask, 'In the flowering days
How did they look?'
We try and make a picture for ourselves,
Fail, and ask the great artists and sculptors,
'How did they look?'

There are countless pictures of Christ our Lord
And his mother,

Statues in stone and wood, stained glass windows,
They tell of some artist's love and longing
But not our own.

Yet some may delight our love of beauty,
Or hold for us
Some truth that helps us in our search for truth.
I think of two pictures of our Lady
That satisfy.

Fra Angelico, friend of the angels,
Painter and saint,
Saw Gabriel and Mary delicate
As flowers, ethereal as rainbows,
Not of this world.

The Spaniard Velasquez, lover of men,
Seeking their depths,
Portrayed our Lady as a peasant girl,
Sturdy and strong, with a grave dignity
And courtesy.

These three wise men, three kings, have come to see
Her new-born son,
To do him honour and present to him
Their strange, rich gifts, brought from a far country
With careful love.

Though she may not understand their coming
She welcomes them
On behalf of her son, and for his sake.
She does not hold him cradled in her arms,
Against her breast,

Her strong hands hold him upright on her knees.
So small a child,
Bound up so stiffly in his swaddling bands,
He surveys the scene with astonishment
But with no fear.

The splendid, rugged faces of the men
About the child,
Their robes, their gifts, are lit with living light;
But the fearless child looks beyond, to where
The night is dark.

One can picture this woman and her son
In their dark hour.
His cross, not her hands, hold him now upright
In love and prayer, arms stretched out to the world
He dies to save.

She is there, a rock of strength beside him,
Without movement,
Frozen by the agony within her
But giving him the last ounce of her strength
To help him through.

Mother Mary, how can we reconcile
These two pictures?
How can that fragile flower of a girl
Be the same woman as the rock of grief?
'They are the same.'

Fra Angelico, that heavenly man,
Was still on earth
When he painted the Annunciation,
But praying he had knelt at heaven's door
And seen its light,

Breathed the clean air of holiness and peace,
Heard faint echoes
Of serene, angelic, perfect music,
Pure voices soaring in adoration;
Love's own dear voice.

How could this poet-painter speak to us
Of what he knew?

In pictures filled with light and purity,
Figures not earthly, symbols of the soul,
Of Mary's soul.

The Spaniard, meditating on the Word,
Looked for it here,
With us in this world of sin and sorrow,
Of war and wounds, disaster and distress,
To which Christ came.

For him the broad hands of a peasant girl
Could be lovely
As the rugged features of toiling man,
For when love looks out through the eyes the flesh
Is glorified.

These two painters, uniting earth and heaven,
Were men of truth.
The woman of toil and grief united
With her delicate spirit is Mary,
Mother of Christ our Lord who is our joy
                                        Now and for ever.


## RAINBOW IN WALES

Not even Turner could have painted
The beauty that I saw that morning,
And who could have described the silence
In which it grew to its perfection?
Of the passing of flame-touched clouds
A painter can give us a shadow,
A symbol, but not the full glory
Of what he has seen, and how can one
Speak of silence without breaking it?

But a few, a selfless music-maker,
A man of prayer, these know that silence,

The music of living light, is known
Only in the stillness of selflessness.
These open their purged hearts in secret
That the music may flow through them
To a tormented world.
Of what the opened heart suffers
Beethoven speaks in his late quartettes,
And thrushes in the quietness of dusk.

We of the unpurged heart, weak in loving,
Knowing nothing, yet long to tell
Of the glories we have seen.
We make our own poor symbols, our treasures,
Strung on the cord of our longing.

But who of us can paint or say or sing
Of what is beyond the glories
That are themselves but symbols?
Yet to search for colours, fumble for words,
Strive to catch in earthly song
The echo of greater music,
To fail with heartbreak and give
The heartbreaks to each other with our love,
Can this be why we live?

And so, inadequate of words,
I can say only that there had been storm
Filling the night with tumult,
And now silence and clear light.
There had been anxiety and fear
And now the half-circle of a rainbow
Flung over the bay, brimming with all the
Colours of white light and resting against
Sky blue as the frail eggshell of a wren.
The sea in its new-born exhausted calm
Lay as the mirror of the sky, and the
Haze of mist left by the storm,
Gentling them both, made of them
One undivided peaceful heaven.

When stillness holds perfection
In the cup of silence time vanishes,
And the watcher's body of time
Seems no longer his habitation.
We can believe the eyes of the soul look,
And will always look, at what will never fade.
Then a gull flew up through the rainbow,
A breath of wind fingered the flawless sea
As though a hand lightly touched the harp-strings,
And a motionless brown speck, a curlew,
Uttered a cry of sorrow.

The rainbow was fading and time came back.
Soul-eyes closed as the eyes of the body
Strained through tears to watch the fading light.
Yet the gull flew on through the blue height
And the last gleam of light on his white wings
Flashed a word back to earth.
'Only the symbols fade.'

Back in the prison of the flesh I found
A mist of rain shrouding the world.
I heard the sandpipers talking, and thought
Came back, and wonder about the rainbow.
Here only the half-circle,
Out of our sight the perfect whole.
Here light fractured into earthly colours,
There the white light of eternity.
And I thought on the Word of God,
Spoken in eternity in silence,
Spoken once in time by one who cried out
The great Word of Love through a perfect life
And a perfect death.
He put off his seamless garment of light
To be with us in our living, and broke
The circle of his being on the cross
To be with us in our dying.

Christ our Word, tell us, what is our sad star,
This speck in the cosmos of creation?
A room full of naughty children,
The nursery of our loving?
Are we here to learn to love as you loved?
Life is so short and we learn so little.
Playing with symbols like children with toys,
We try to learn, and fail, and break our hearts
Because we fail.
But we give you our heartbreaks with our love
And that is why we live.


## TO OUR PLUM TREES IN WINTER

*(There is a painting by one of the Old Masters which shows
a dead body lying on a bier. Behind the bier stands Christ
holding a baby in his arms – the new-born soul)*

Never unknown to us, old trees,
Always a part of our loving
Since the old house first took us to itself,
Turning us east to face the new beginning,
Promising peace that was not withheld.
For how long have you leaned there by the hedge,
Supplicating the winter sunrise
To come soon, begging for warmth and light
And the honour to hold through one more spring
The silver blossoms and the golden songs.

How old are you, beloved trees?
Were you young when the house was built,
Timber-framed and claiming kinship with you;
Trees, holy ones, home-makers for all who come.
So confident then in fearless youth,
Now sorely afraid in your brittle age
Of the crash in the dark and no more spring.

The wind plucks from your heart-strings the cry of
   grief.
In the fine tracery of your branches,
The queen moon alight in your twisted age.
Is it sorrow to be crowned with so much light?

Take heart for there is another music.
Time, the old spinning-woman, is at her wheel,
Singing softly, laughing at your fears and mine.
'Living is loving and giving, my dears,
And death is re-birth to give again.
The sun to whom you gave your gift of love
Gives his to you to live in your old bones.
Re-born as the old oaks that make the house
You shall glow in winter-warmth upon the hearth,
Flower-flame to give light in darkness,
Light fair as the glimmer of moon and stars
That once you held so proudly.
When the petals are fallen to soft ash
Men dare to say, "The fire is dead." They lie.
The City of God is built of sacrifice.'

So the old spinning woman comforts the trees,
And comforts us, tender midwife that she is,
Knowing our fear of sacrificial change.
For time's a midwife, withdrawing from the womb
The threads of being that are her care till death.
Constant as our heart-beat, faithful as our breath,
We hardly think of her until the heart-beat
Falters, the breath fails, and we plead with her,
'Old nurse, always with me, do not leave me.
Keep your foot upon the treadle.
Do not take your hands away.'

'Death is re-birth,' she reminds us. 'It was from
Your mother's womb I lifted you into life
And you cried to go back to your safe darkness,
So why weep when I lift you there again?

Lie in its gentleness at peace,
The growing light a song of safety.
And then, oh my dears, the gently lifting hands
Whose touch is joy! No, not my hands
That lift you, for time is earth-bound,
But the pierced hands of love that uphold all things.'

So time comforts the children, for their sakes
Keeping her worn old face serene and still
That she may banish fear and give them peace.
Yet in the storm-music of that night
Was great and weary sorrow,
And in a moment of strange silence
The grief pierced through me like a sword.
'My children, remember me in your bliss,
For I am weary of the treadle.
Too long have I laboured at my wheel.
How long, oh Lord, how long? Have mercy.
Let time be lost in your eternity.'


## OLD AGE

They say Christ knows all our sorrows
Since he himself passed through each one.
They are pearls on a golden chain,
And hidden at the heart of each
We find the gold of his presence.
'That's not true,' said one old person.
'Christ did not live to be old.'
No, but which way would you have it?
Mothers, losing their only sons,
Have remembered, Christ too died young,
And knowing their sons honoured by
His shining company, found peace.
Would you take that comfort from them?

Or could you endure to picture
The splendour of the Holy Mount
Fading away through the shadows
Of failing powers and dusty death?
Better by far the lightning stroke
Of quick disaster, met with a
Stark royalty of courage.
One moonlit night of treachery,
Daylight hours of shame and tumult,
Pain burning with the speed of flame.
Then sunset and a holy death,
Dark night, and dawn bringing knowledge
That God's love is young forever.

But he did know about old age,
For is not the Way of Sorrows
A picture of it? Christina
Rossetti asked sadly, 'And does
The road wind uphill all the way?'
If you go to Jerusalem
You can see yourself that it does.
And sometimes old people break down
Under the weight of arthritis,
Cancer, or whatever burden
They must bear, and they are ashamed.
They need not be for Christ himself
Fell under the weight he carried.

And they do not want to be helped.
Christ, when he fell, accepted help.
Loving Simon for what he did
His humility would have left
No room in his mind for hurt pride.
What filled his mind as he toiled on,
Uphill through mockery and hate?
Anguish filled it, not for himself
But for his beloved people
When there came on them that event

Of which he had foreknowledge, the
Fall of Jerusalem and the
Agony of its destruction.
To the women weeping for him
He said 'Weep not for me but weep
For our city and her children.'

He had wept over the city
Himself, crying out in sorrow,
'Jerusalem, Jerusalem,
How often would I have gathered
Your children together, as the
Mother hen gathers her chickens
Under her wings, and you would not.'

Oh the agony in God's heart
When we choose our selfish evil
And mock and deny his goodness.
With his sunlight on our faces
We turn into the cold darkness
Of our own shadow; and blame him
For our chosen desolation.

We are those weeping women, we
Who are old. For tears can be prayer,
And prayer ends often in weeping.
We are Simeon and Anna
Living out our last days in the
Stillness of the house of prayer.
Humbly he will come to us there,
As he came to them on the day
When Mary's child was lifted up
To God and the sword pierced her heart.
When our prayer is marked with his
Cross of pain then we know we are
In his glorious company.

# EASTER IN THE WARD

Tomorrow it would be Easter Day.
Beyond the high hospital windows
There must be a freshness in the world;
Trees unfurling their dear April green,
The doves calling, kingcups by the stream,
White violets scenting the hedgerows.

The windows showed only stark chimneys.
The hot and crowded ward held much pain,
Many uncomforted tragedies.
Day and night they came in, lying still
On the stretchers, shocked and much afraid.
Cars and lorries passed but no birds sang.

If only they could be comforted!
The gypsy girl, battered by hard blows,
Struggling out of her bed to run away.
'Lie still, dear,' we would say. 'You are safe.
Lie down again.' But she could not rest.
She must run from the blows and escape.

And another girl, comely and brave.
Her boy's motor cycle, wildly swerving
Had crashed them both against a lorry.
Would she walk again? No one could know.
Broken limbs strung up on traction
She laughed and was sure she would get well.

Not all sadness. By day there were joys.
Sister competent, serenely kind.
Young nurses, mostly kind, sometimes not,
But good to look at, full of laughter.
Pots of bright flowers, shafts of sunlight,
Small children visiting Mum or Gran.

But there seemed no comfort for the old:
So old myself, how I ached for them.
'You do not know what I have suffered'
Said one. She was right. Pain is private.
'What would my poor husband say if he
Could see me now?' another asked me.

They all feared the geriatric ward
As once old people feared the workhouse,
A place from which you never come out.
I was ashamed, safe home behind me.
I prayed. 'Christ, have mercy on the old.'
Why was he not here to comfort them?

Ours is now, they say, a heathen land.
The ward had not noticed Good Friday.
Would we remember Easter morning?
'We used to,' said a nurse I had asked.
'We used to sing hymns in the chapel.
Lovely, it was, we don't do it now.'

She spoke sadly, for she was sorry.
If only he would come tomorrow,
Despite our ignoring of his cross,
Walk down the ward in the living light
Of resurrection glory, what then?
There would be none left uncomforted.

I could not sleep that night, wanting him.
The ward was strangely quiet, peaceful
As it seldom was. No accidents,
No distress, moaning or restlessness.
Yet I felt no peace and prayed to die,
Lest I should burden those who loved me.

A clock struck. Midnight. A new day born.
Easter morning and I prayed for death.
'To die into your resurrection.'

Could one ask for any greater gift?
I asked for it again and again.
'To die into your resurrection.'

The hours passed and there was no answer.
Dawn came and with it a line of verse.
'The shining silence of the scorn of God.'
But the poet was mistaken there,
Our courteous Lord was never scornful
And silence can be love's still small voice,

Asking that we should wait a moment,
Accepting from him the proffered gift
Of his own everlasting patience . . .
Yes, but for us his divine moments
Seem an eternity of waiting.
When, merciful love? When will you come?

Full dawn now. What was that joyous noise?
Trumpets of the dawn? Easter trumpets?
No, a dear familiar clattering,
A musical clinking and ringing.
Heads lifted from hot pillows. There was
Hope and expectation in the ward.

It was Ida with the tea trolley,
Dear black Ida, rattling and banging,
Swaying and singing down the long ward.
Like a ship in full sail was Ida,
Crying aloud the tidings of joy.
'Cup of tea with sugar? With sugar?'

Her proportions were large as her heart,
Her eyes and teeth flashed in her dark face
As she flung back her head in laughter,
Singing, most days, snatches of old songs
Interwoven with that joyous cry,
'Cup of tea with sugar? Sugar?'

Her singing voice, deep and glorious,
Had a new power this Easter Day.
Not snatches of song but melody
Sustained and unified, ecstatic.
I could not hear the words and asked her,
'Ida, what is it you are singing?'

Her deep voice was bell-like with her joy
As she cried out for us all to hear,
'I'm singing to my Lord Jesus Christ!'
So, on Easter morning, he had come.
The great teapot became a Chalice
And the sugar basin a Paten.

The risen sun filled the ward with light,
We held out our hands for his bounty.


## THE HUMMINGBIRDS' NEST

I have a treasure from a far country,
A delicate cup of woven grasses
It stands upright upon a small brown twig.
Two bright hummingbirds made it together,
A nest for lovers, a cradle for their babes,
Lined with white cotton soft as a cloud.

In it the mother laid her snow-white eggs,
Almost too small to be seen but jewels
Beyond price to the gallant beating hearts
Hidden beneath the feathers of pure gold;
And to the love that made the bright-eyed stars,
The flowers and the rustling leaves of spring.

And, once more, the miracle came to pass
And new life stirred under the mother's heart.
The first cheep was heard and then the nestlings came,

Greeting each dawn with clamorous hunger
And crocus-coloured, wide, demanding mouths.
Only at sunset were they satisfied.

Only then would they shut their open mouths
And settle to sweet sleep beneath the warmth
Of their mother's golden quilt of feathers.
Proudly she covered them with her glory,
Proudly, in his crimson coat, their father
Toiled from dawn to dusk to calm their hunger.

He was one of many darting jewels
Of small birds cleaving the hot, bright sunshine
And clear sky with arrows of swift flight.
They would have seemed more butterfly than bird
But for the long, sharp scimitars of beaks
Balanced by a cornet's tail of feathers.

The birds were gleams of love in the blue air
Of days of such unbroken calm they seemed
To hold the promise of eternity.
No storms, no fear of darkness, no terror
Of winged evil could this year break their joy.
This year, all would be rounded into peace.

But in this world we have the promises,
Not their fulfilment. A hot stifling night
Brought rain, a rumbling of coming thunder,
A dark veiling of the luminous stars.
Only a tropical storm, but such things
Can hold great dangers for the innocent.

They bring the black-winged evil predators
Striking like the lightning out of darkness,
And sly beasts of prey, creeping silently.
This is the horn of the evil powers
Who love darkness. Only the rising sun
Can banish them and show what they have done.

A finger of light, shining through wet leaves,
Touched with compassion the gallant upright
Nest upon its twig. For it was empty.
Scattered feathers, like torn flower petals,
Could say only of the small, bright birds that
They had died silently and together.

The nest in its forsaken emptiness,
Seemed now a miniature microcosm
Of the eternal heartbreak of the world.
And yet it still stood upright on its twig,
Denying emptiness and proclaiming
Silently its gift of hidden treasure.

Travelling over the curve of the world,
The leagues of the sea, it came home at last,
As a gift of love for an old woman,
To a glass cabinet holding treasures
Of a lifetime; small things, cups and saucers,
Shells, birds and beasts of ivory and glass.

Bigger than these, the nest upon its twig
Watched over them with kindliness. Empty
Only to the eye but full of living
Memories of light and warmth and colour,
Crimson and azure, purple and soft gold,
The whisper of leaves spelling out blessing.

The children, when the nest was shown to them,
Were speechless with wonder as their fingers
Explored carefully the rounded softness
Of the white cotton lining, and their eyes
Were wide and bright as imagination
Saw birds like jewels flashing through the air.

There is an eternity in beauty
That death is never able to destroy.
The gentlest things, the frailest, are not lost.

Transmuted into happy dreams, perhaps.
Memories, intimations of great peace,
They are with us still.


## THE DREAM

That night happy dreams led up step by step
To the humble threshold of the great dream,
And they were linked as on a chain, dreams of
Home but too far back for clear remembrance.
Rainbow-misted with soft flower colours,
Haunted with the music of unseen birds;
Autumnal beauty held them charmed and still.

In some of these gardens I walked alone,
Knowing that in these dreams I touched only
The fringe of reality, the garden
Only, not the home itself. Once I saw
A glimmer of light in a windowpane,
A warm patch of red brick. And once a door.
I stretched out my hand, longing to go in,
Then drew it back. Entrance was forbidden.

For it was locked on deep-down memories.
Recalled they would confuse my present days.
And there was no key upon the outside.
I could no more unlock it than I could
Unlock that door within my soul that led
To the holy place lit by the flower
Of Pentecost, the bright flame of God's love.
It could be opened only from within.

But in other dreams I was not alone,
A much-loved companion was with me.
I could feel his presence, see his shadow
As he came to me over the green grass,

Lean peacefully against his love for me,
But never could I look into his eyes
Or catch even the echoes of his voice.
Yet I knew he was there and was content.

One day, I knew, I should see him clearly,
Feel his arms about me and hear his voice,
Find we were no strangers to each other
But two companions from long love made one.
Hand in hand we would go to the locked door
And find it had been unlocked from within.
We would go in and gather together
The shining threads of a perfected love.

Between these dreams, and that to which they led,
There was the threshold dream, not elusive,
Not rainbow misted but clear and simple.
A bed in a small room and to the right
Curtains drawn across the night's deep darkness.
The woman of the dreams, myself, old now,
Lay in the bed motionless and waiting.
The parting curtains would bring night; then dawn.

That threshold picture vanished quickly,
Washed away by a wave of black darkness.
When I woke I was standing on the shore
Of a dark forest. I had passed through it
And like an ebbing tide it left me there,
Amazed and yet most peacefully at home.
At my feet flowers were bright with welcome
And over us the sky was sunrise gold.

Then, oh then, I felt the Presence with me
At my left, but at some little distance,
A cloaked figure, the hood hiding his face,
Stood motionless, a figure of still peace
And gentle dignity. Yet how alive
He was! The glory of the rising sun

Was his, the colours of the morning sky,
The life of the unfolding flower buds.

There was a stirring now of happy birds,
Sweet clear trills of music that would soon grow
Into an outflowing of ecstasy.
A hidden stream ran laughing secretly,
Making music over the mossy stones.
They sang aloud to him whose love created them
To cry aloud his own clear Word of love
Who is himself the Word, their only life.

And my life too, for I was born again
In this symbolic dawning of my dream,
Sin, pain and sorrow left behind me now
In the darkness that was slipping from me.
'I go to prepare a place for you,' he said.
A place for sinners to begin again
To love and serve each other for his sake.
I thought, 'If only I could see his face.'

How could I? Such a glory must be earned.
A saint, beholding his glory unveiled,
Fell at his feet as one dead. Seeing him
Clothed in light upon the mountain his friends
Trembled and were exceedingly afraid
Until he came himself to comfort them.
Even in dream I could not go to him,
But even in dream he could come to me.

How can I tell of it? There are no words
Except his own words spoken long ago,
When he spoke of his longing to gather
His chickens under his wings. How often
Have I tried to do just what he wanted,
To run and run and hide under his wings
And nestle close to his warm heart of love.
But, a sinner, I could not find the way.

'Come unto me,' he said, but now he came
To me. Always the symbols. He himself,
On earth, used them in his teaching of us,
And in the life here they are our treasure,
There, blind-eyed as kittens, we may need them
Until soul-eyes open on the real.
And so I thought that a fold of his cloak
Came round me with exquisite tenderness,

Soft as a cloud, as light as air, until
A gleam of sunshine like happy laughter
Lit the transparent feathers to rainbow
Loveliness. I felt their delicate touch
And a joy too great for a dream to hold
Shattered the dream, and I woke to sorrow.
Only a dream, but never forgotten
It shines in the dark like the morning star.

One's own words are poor things, so this book shall end . . . not with my own fumbling . . . it shall end with Thomas Traherne rejoicing in the glory of love.

O God, who by love alone art great and glorious, that art present and livest with us by love alone: Grant us likewise by love to attain another self, by love to live in others, and by love to come to our glory, to see and accompany Thy love throughout all eternity.

*The Joy of the Snow*